BOOZERS, BALLCOCKS
& BAIL

ABOUT THE AUTHOR

After entering the profession 'by default', Steve Smith worked his way up from office boy's assistant ('my first job was to blow up a rugby ball for the senior partner's son') to co-founder of the criminal law practice Wilford Smith, based in Rotherham in South Yorkshire.

Boozers, Ballcocks & Bail – the first book in Steve's comic legal series – was originally self-published, and said to be 'the most shoplifted book in Yorkshire'.

A professional public speaker in his spare time, Steve is married with a daughter and lives in Rotherham. He was awarded an MBE in the 2006 Queen's Birthday Honours List for his services to charity, and is president of Rotherham Town Cricket Club.

Sample chapters of other books in the series available at:
www.steve-d-smith.co.uk

BOOZERS, BALLCOCKS & BAIL

Stephen D. Smith

Neville Douglas Publishing Ltd

Published in 2006 by Neville Douglas Publishing Ltd, Barnsley,
South Yorkshire, S73 0LY

10 9 8 7 6 5 4 3 2

A CIP catalogue record for this book is available from the British Library

Printed and bound in Great Britain by LPPS Ltd

ISBN 10: 0-901853-77-2 ISBN 13: 978-1-901853-77-3

Visit Steve Smith at www.steve-d-smith.co.uk

Represented by Signature Book Services

To Jennifer and Rebecca with love

CONTENTS

FOREWORD

There are certain people who have added immeasurably to the quality of my life: loving parents, my wife Christine and my four children, teachers with shining eyes, my editor at Penguin, and many more. And then there are writers like Steve Smith, who has delighted and entertained me with his stories of life as a criminal lawyer in a northern industrial town.

At a time when the publishing world is flooded with misery memoirs, it is refreshing to find books which lift the spirit and make the reader laugh out loud. And it is important to have books which make us laugh out loud, for laughter, the psychologists tell us, is good for us; it increases our immunity to illness, improves sleep and enhances our lives. Steve Smith's books certainly do.

These aren't merely collections of funny tales: there is depth and quality to the writing. Here is an author who has blended hilarious anecdote with the most poignant and sometimes quite heart-rending descriptions of life on the wrong side of the law. He has peopled his vividly realised books with a rich tapestry of compelling characters – the incompetent, the foolish, the pathetic, the cruel, the vulnerable and the downright bizarre – all of whom are brought to life in richly comic and sometimes tragic situations.

Gervase Phinn

PREFACE

This book is an account of my life as a criminal lawyer in Rotherham. Not all cases are chronicled here; I have picked out some of the more interesting ones.

My memoirs are based on true events but in some cases the names of the characters have been changed to respect privacy.

I always wanted to be a professional musician but my parents forced me to get a 'proper' job – rightly – so I got employment as an office boy's assistant at a firm of solicitors, an auspicious start to my legal career. Over the next few years I continued with this temporary job, attending night school on the way.

Eventually I qualified as a solicitor, and two years later formed my own practice. I gave up my musical aspirations to concentrate on working in one of the great professions.

This is where my story starts…

ACKNOWLEDGEMENTS

I would like to thank my friends for appearing in this book and supporting me throughout my life.

I would also like to acknowledge the incredible contribution made to my career and life by my long-suffering family, and I dearly wish that my mother, father, brother Neville and his wife Heather had lived to see this book see the light of day.

I am indebted to Christine and Gervase Phinn, whose support and advice has been incalculable. Gervase gave me the confidence to persevere with the book and for that I am truly grateful.

I would also like to thank Susanne McDadd of Publishing Services and Cathy Douglas, without whom we would never have got this far – Susanne for the benefit of her patience, understanding and support and skill in producing this book, and Cathy for taking my manuscript and turning it into a readable text that even I can understand.

Also thanks to Barbara Bramhall, The Ernest Booth Trio, Graham 'Bodger' Broom, Neil Crossland, Lewis 'the mad Scotsman' Frame, Christopher 'Goody' Good, Michael Jarvis, Peter Large, David 'Bader' Lidster, Jenni Morton, Tim 'Ten-Belly' Norburn, Sean 'Pagey' Page, Mick Smallwood, Wilfred Steer Q.C., Michael Walker, Leslie Walton, Martin Ward, Steven F. Wilford and Albert, one of my most loyal clients.

And finally, thanks to Don Morton, Tom 'the Hemingfield Fusilier' Furniss, Gillian Furniss, and my long-suffering secretary Michelle Fisher.

ONE

ALBERT AND A LOAD OF BALLCOCKS

The day we opened Wilford Smith, my first client was Jack Heptonstall, a likeable rogue with a weakness for other people's property. He had never committed a house burglary or robbed an old person – as he put it, he avoided 'Joe Public' – but scrapyards and commercial properties were fair game. Jack had a flair for driving whilst disqualified, and in all the years he'd been a driver, I don't think he was ever insured. He had nine children, and when I once asked him why so many, he told me that he'd never owned a television. All his children had inherited the huge grin that dominated his face – along with his faults. There are certain clients you can't help liking, and Jack and his family were among them.

Jack, who had come to ask me to represent him at Rotherham Magistrates' Court the following day, had brought along his youngest son, about seven years old. Albert was a spotty little urchin with an appealing, almost angelic, face that belied his nature, as I found out when he picked up a bottle of ink from my desk and spilt it all over my papers. Jack clouted him about the ear, called him a 'twat', and told him to be quiet. Within seconds the lad was checking to see if my plastic telephone would split if propelled with great force against the desk. Another clout ensued, whereupon the little boy shouted, 'Gi' ower!'

'Oh, it can speak,' I thought, as Albert began to pick his nose.

Throughout the visit, he stared at me with an unreadable

smile. Jack's cup of tea arrived together with a glass of squash for the boy; Albert managed to knock over the tea, which crept along my file under the legal aid application I'd just filled in and into my top left-hand drawer. Significantly, he didn't waste a drop of his drink. The boy was a disaster area. How I kept my temper I don't know, but I was placated to some extent by Jack's continual clouts.

As our meeting was about to finish, I was aghast to see the brat standing on a chair, trying to capture the koi carp in our fish tank. 'Put the bugger back, you little bastard!' shouted his father with annoyance, clouting him again.

'Yes, put the bugger back, you little bastard,' I echoed, with even greater annoyance.

'Gi' ower,' said the boy. 'Gi' ower, will tha? That's child abuse!' Jack clouted him again, twice. 'No, *that's* child abuse.'

I got up, took the fish's castle from Albert and put it back in the tank, at which point one of the carp bit me. My immediate reaction was to pull my arm out of the way, only to splash the front of my immaculately ironed white shirt with water and streaks of green algae, which burrowed into the cotton. In a mere forty minutes, one small boy had almost destroyed my brand new office and image.

'Anyway, we'll get off now,' said Jack. 'Come on, son, say goodbye to Steve.'

'Tarra Steve,' said the boy, offering his hand. I shook it, and came into contact with something extremely sticky. Albert had donated me his used chewing gum.

He laughed, then turned to follow his father, who was blissfully unaware of what the little shit had done. 'Well, Albert,' I thought, 'I'll certainly remember you.'

I had worked in the law since 1965, coming to Rotherham in 1971. At night school I qualified as a Fellow of the Institute of Legal Executives, which I used as a springboard to become a solicitor of the Supreme Court in 1979. I joined a local firm as assistant solicitor and two years later, achieved my ambition of opening my own practice.

I joined forces with my friend and colleague Steven Wilford, who would deal with conveyancing, probate and non-contentious matters, and look after the money, while I dealt with the contentious court proceedings. We'd started work at the same firm and got on well, so kept in touch after I left. In 1973 my then employers were looking for someone about my age who worked in land law and conveyancing; I suggested Wilf, and was delighted when they took him on. He's a remarkable character, a gifted lawyer and excellent office manager, who also likes a drink (as do I and most of our friends!). We were a good match, I the extrovert and Wilford the stable one, and despite all the problems and doubts, the scheme was as exciting as anything I had ever been involved in.

By early January 1981 we had acquired our office; we rented the ground floor to a small print shop, and the upper floors were to be shared between Wilford Smith and Co., Solicitors of Rotherham, South Yorkshire, and our friend Michael Jarvis, an accountant, who needed a room because of overcrowding in his own offices. I met Michael in 1971, when he was working on the books of my then employers, and we hit it off immediately. A ginger-haired, chubby man with an athletic frame – he even played table-tennis for his county – he's easy-going and well and truly 'one of the boys'. The nicest compliment I can pay him is that I've never heard anybody say a bad word about him. He's also an extremely able accountant, who never lets his socialising skills get in the way of his profession! We would be the town's tenth firm of solicitors, and were due to open in May with a staff of one. The premises were dilapidated, with holes in the roof and a recalcitrant ballcock in the loo that liked to shoot out of the cistern and hit you on the side of the head while simultaneously showering you with water. But it would be our own.

On my next free evening I took my family to see the premises, probably more of a thrill for me than for them. While my mother, wife and daughter explored, my father set about mending the ballcock. After much effort and some swearing, he sat back on the toilet seat flushed (sorry!) with success. 'Shouldn't be a problem now, son,' he said, pulling the chain to demonstrate. The ballcock promptly hit him on the back of the head as water shot out of the bowl, soaking the seat of his pants. I rocked with laughter, and after a few seconds he joined in. He laughed so much that he began to cough, sweat running down his temples as he held his sides in an attempt to relieve himself of a stitch. For the rest of the evening, as we cleared up and discussed decor, I could hear him chuckling in the background, reliving the incident.

During the following weeks the whole family joined in: my wife Jennifer, father, mother, and six-year-old daughter Rebecca – who once accidentally kicked over a bucket of emulsion, causing my father even greater hilarity when Wilford slipped in it and gave his Levis a magnificent cream patch around his bottom. Their efforts were such that our two rooms were quickly cleaned and beautifully decorated. We got hold of some second-hand furniture from a dealer in Sheffield, and bought two brand-new desks, one for reception (the larger room, where Anne, our one member of staff, would answer the phone, attend to visitors and do her typing), and one for the office Wilford and I would share. Looking back, I suppose it was a bit of a hovel, but to us it was a dream come true.

About a week before we were due to open, our brass plate arrived, bearing the names of the firm and the two partners, and I rushed to my parents' house to show it to my father, who was delighted. The following day, my mate Graham Broom, joiner-cum-builder-cum-entrepreneur, affectionately nicknamed Bodger for his skills, came to fix it outside our office door. Having done so, he asked me to come out and check it. He had mounted it upside down, and I pretended I hadn't noticed. We had a good laugh, he made the necessary adjustment, and the job was done. It looked immaculate.

I later picked up Jennifer and Rebecca and my parents, and drove the whole family to Rotherham to show them the name-plate. This was one of the most moving moments of my life. My father had always been in awe of the legal profession – the only time he ever went to see a solicitor he wore his best suit, smelling of mothballs – so the fact that his son had achieved his own office gave him immense pleasure. As he looked at my name on the brass plate he wiped away a tear, and to conceal his emotion, brought out a camera to record it. (I later found out he'd forgotten to put a film in it, so all the effort was for nothing.)

A day or two later Jarvis moved in his VAT department, con-sisting of his friend Oscar, a genius at VAT who unfortunately suffered from dreadful flatulence, becoming quite famous in local circles for his ability to break wind almost on demand. He was also extremely keen on draught Guinness, which I am convinced aggravated his problem. He had a room of his own and a share of the toilet, which was at the top of the stairs.

Oscar was the most consistent person I knew in everything he did, not least his ablutions. He had his breakfast and a cigarette at the same time, bought the same paper from the same news-vendor and walked the same route to the same office, each and every day. The downside to this rigid regime was his dreadful problems each morning, not later than 9.45am, when he took his first major visit to the lavatory. He always took the *Racing News* with him: a keen horse-racing enthusiast, Oscar liked to consider the day's form whilst he sat doing his duty. The area had to be avoided like the plague, and was.

In the last few days before we opened we were busy with the final arrangements. We had to register with the Law Society and legal aid board, as well as informing the local building societies and banks of our move, in the hope they might give us some work. Although both of us had been in Rotherham for about ten years and had built up some business relationships, and indeed a clientele on the litigation side, we now had to start bringing in business for Wilford Smith and Co.

As we got nearer the day, all the financial details were put into place. I'd borrowed £2,500 from my parents, and Wilford the same from his mother. Some of it had gone to buy office equipment, and on deposits for the two cars we'd bought. The rest was in the bank as a buffer against wages and day-to-day expenses. We were indeed working on a shoestring.

The grand opening was 13 May 1981, and in the days leading up to it we received a great deal of help from our friends in the business community. Wilford had taken a couple of weeks' holiday, but I was still working out my notice, though most lunchtimes were spent at the new office. One such lunchtime I went to deliver some stationery, and found that Oscar was paying his second visit of the day to the loo. We were aware that he was in there, because the toilet adjoined our office and the walls were thin.

As we finished our business, Oscar finished his. I could have sworn that I heard him cursing, but thought nothing of it. We were leaving our room as he too emerged, rubbing the side of his head.

'Good afternoon, Oscar, any winners today?'

'Oh hello, lads, not today,' he said distractedly, and disappeared into his office.

'Did you see the lump on the side of his head?' Wilford asked.

'Why don't we get a plumber in?' I asked earnestly, and we both burst out laughing. The ballcock had struck again.

I left my old job on Friday 8 May, after ten happy years with the firm, to become a self-employed solicitor in Rotherham. Over the weekend, I rang all my friends with the new number.

When the big day came, with no files, an empty diary, but a lot of hope, I set off for work bright and early, calling at a local shop for milk – we had agreed that the first week would be my turn for the collection rota. (This was just one example of the decisions self-employed business partners have to make.) On my way I met one of the local prosecutors, Philip Chadwick, walking towards the court. Seeing the bottles in each hand, and knowing that I had left my old job, he shouted to me, 'That's a good idea until you get established, a little milk round.' I laughed. Nothing was going to upset or offend me that day.

At the office, someone had stuck a balloon to our front door, bearing the words 'Happy Birthday Margaret'. I couldn't believe Sean Page had been up so early that morning! (Our friend the Honourable Sean Page, insurance broker and all-round good egg, is one of those characters who can brighten any dull occasion with his wit – or more accurately, lunacy.)

I opened up and went in, and soon Wilford appeared, carrying two bottles of Newcastle Brown Ale. I presumed they would be part of our lunch, but I was wrong: they were part of *his* lunch. Anne appeared a few minutes later, carrying a bottle of champagne. 'What a lovely gesture,' I said, only to be told that it was to be *her* lunch! We weren't having that, and opened the bottle there and then.

At 9am the phone started to ring, with calls from well-wishers. We even had some post: one letter confirming that we had been entered onto the legal aid panel, the rest greetings cards. Page's bore the legend 'A happy Easter to all of you'.

By 10am the fuss had died down, and all the post been opened. Wilford and I sat across the desk from each other and suddenly faced the realisation that we had nothing to do. Wilford Smith was open for business, but had none.

'I know!' said Wilford. 'Pass me the screwdriver. There's one job I can do; that damn ballcock.'

But before he could set about it, the phone rang again. It was a local estate agent, asking if we were interested in dealing with a house transaction for one of his clients. This was Wilford's department, and he enthusiastically took down the details of our very first job.

'I can see them right now if you want, I'm free at the moment,' he said, and within half an hour our first clients came through the door. I suppose we overdid it, for they not only got an interview with Wilford, but one with me and our secretary, plus copious amounts of coffee from a donated percolator that burnt your fingers every time you used it. They went away happily carrying our business cards, a list of our services, our emergency number and a potted history of the firm and its partners. Their transaction was completed in record time, and to our delight, only a few days later they brought in a relative who was also buying a house.

We spent the rest of the morning showing friends round the premises, then at lunchtime went to the Cross Keys and advertised ourselves to all and sundry for an hour and a quarter. By 2.15pm we were back in the office, and found Jack Heptonstall waiting to see me. Wilford Smith and Co. was up and running.

TWO

THE DAY THE BANKER CAME TO CALL

We did extremely well in our first month. We were lucky; all sorts of work arrived from unexpected quarters, and our friends in the business community put a considerable amount our way.

One Monday morning Wilford arrived, excited because the manager of the local branch of the Halifax Building Society, one of the largest in Rotherham, wanted to call to see how we were getting on. Jack Bower was a very important person, in a position to provide mortgages and put a lot of conveyancing work our way – and even more importantly, at the stroke of a pen he could alter the course of our overdraft! Wilford had met him often, and enjoyed an excellent rapport with him.

Wilf arranged the appointment for noon the following Friday, having confirmed that I would be there too, as I had a light court that day. We agreed that the office should be in pristine condition, and decided to buy a new coffee-maker and half a dozen china cups and saucers – Oscar had tipped Shergar to win the Derby, and we'd had a successful flutter. Anne was sent out to make the purchases while Wilford managed the office, answered the phone, made the tea and tackled the ballcock, which had broken again.

We had three days to prepare for the visit, but nature was against us. As the weather became very warm, the flutterings in the roof increased with the pigeon population, and we were also plagued by the invasion of a small yellow beetle-like creature – in drawers, and on the ceilings, floors and desks. In the uncarpeted areas, they crunched underfoot. The problem was so marked that even Oscar commented on it.

On Wednesday afternoon, Wilford was interviewing a client whose chair was placed directly under the ceiling light when he noticed that the wire from the ceiling to the bulb appeared to be moving. Putting on his glasses, he saw a family of beetles marching down the wire to the lowest point of the bulb whence, lemming-like, they leapt to the floor.

Unfortunately, directly between the light and the floor was Mr Granville Entwhistle, discussing the purchase of his council house.

Wilford watched in agony as the first of the family landed on Granville's shoulder. Others followed; Granville was soon covered in beetles, and Wilford began to feel hot under the collar, in a quandary over what to do. Should he say, 'Please move, Mr Entwhistle, you're infested with beetles from our roof,' or usher him out and hope he'd think he'd acquired his infestation elsewhere? As a man of honour with every care for his clients, he decided to usher him out. He breathed a huge sigh of relief as, watching from the window, Wilford saw Granville disappear, scratching his head and neck frantically.

On Thursday Rentokil came to call, and identified the insects as golden spider beetles, which fed on the waste matter of pigeons. The pigeons' home in the rafters had also been their cemetery, where the infestation had started. We watched in silence as plastic sack after sack was taken away. I still shudder to think of it. The entire roof and floor were sprayed with a golden-spider-beetle deterrent, and we vowed to get the roof repaired before the pigeons returned.

On Friday, we busily prepared for Mr Bower's visit. If he were sufficiently impressed, he would see to it that we were given what was known as 'Solicitor free work', so his visit was very important.

A few seconds before noon, Jack walked into reception, his timing immaculate as always. We welcomed him enthusiastically, poured him a cup of his favourite Darjeeling tea in a brand new bone-china cup, and ushered him into our office. Given that he had a staff of over eighty and offices with all mod cons, he must have wondered what he'd got himself into when he saw our little enterprise. However, he seemed genuinely pleased for us, and was clearly impressed with our attempt to give it a go.

The interview lasted about twenty minutes, and ended with his promise of support for the future. He had no fears about the quality of our work, because Wilford was a brilliant conveyancer and Jack knew it. As we chatted at the top of the stairs, Oscar appeared for his midday visit. 'Excuse me,' he said; Jack moved out of the way, and the toilet door opened. I looked at Wilford.

It wouldn't do to go into graphic details, but suffice it to say that Oscar was on form, and the acoustics added to the agony of the moment. 'It's the VAT inspector,' I told Jack, for want of a better explanation.

'He's got a real problem, that chap,' said Jack as we walked downstairs. We both nodded in agreement.

The following Wednesday morning I set off for the office in pouring rain, the almost black sky illuminated by streaks of lightning. By the time I'd got from the house to the car, my coat was saturated. I had my briefcase and files for the morning, together with my football kit – which should have included two boots, but I realised I'd only brought one. I cursed, rushed back to the house, and found the boot in the passageway. Back in the car, having been soaked again, I found that I had only one football sock. I decided to borrow one from Lidster rather than get soaked again, and drove off.

My interest in football began at school, and continued in adulthood. Wednesday evenings were taken up with matches on the all-weather pitch at the Herringthorpe Leisure Centre in Rotherham. It was a 6pm kick-off, and our team included some very good footballers. They weren't all lawyers, because we had to bring in outsiders to bolster the numbers, and one of them, a lad called David Lidster, was not only our captain and a skills player, but also the main supplier of kit when I'd forgotten mine.

It was an eventful day, because my best client Jack Heptonstall was before the court that morning to be sentenced for theft of lead and driving whilst disqualified. I parked the car and ran to the office, getting drenched for a third time in the process. I'd just started to go through my letters when I felt water dripping onto my head from the area of the light bulb above me. I rushed to turn off the lights so I wouldn't be electrocuted, and went up to investigate the attic: water was dripping into two areas. We used all the buckets and pans we had, one of them perched rather precariously on my desk.

When Wilford came in, soaking wet and cursing the weather, he saw me peering into the bucket to check the contents. 'You must have had a good night,' he announced.

'It's for a leak, you chuff,' I said irritably.

'Why don't you leak in the toilet like everybody else?' he said. I granted him a smile and he sat down opposite me, gazing at the water dripping from the ceiling. He had been sitting only a matter of seconds before he realised that his chair was also saturated. 'Bloody marvellous. Look at this,' he said, pointing to the wet patch round his backside.

'Must have been a good night last night, then,' I said.

'Oh bugger off,' said Wilford. 'What are we going to do about this?' As I had four cases that morning and had to be at court early, we agreed to get Bodger Broom in to see if he could effect some speedy repairs.

After we'd been through the post, Wilf set about trying to persuade Bodger to get out of bed and answer the phone. He let the phone ring and ring and ring.

'Who the bloody hell is that?' I heard Bodger shout.

Wilf couldn't resist shouting 'Wrong number,' and putting the phone down. I then rang Bodger, pretending to be the registrar at the local crematorium.

'Who's booked me in then?' he said furiously. 'I tell thee, I'm not dead!' he shouted, sounding like a man about to die from a stroke. I put the phone down and Wilford then rang him again. By this time, Broomy must have been frothing at the mouth, he was so angry.

He asked Wilford if we'd been messing about, but Wilford denied all knowledge of the other calls, and told him about our roof problem. Broomy said he'd call at lunchtime and bring his hammer. The hammer was probably for Wilford, but as I wouldn't be in I didn't really care.

I set off for court and got soaked again. In the little WRVS tearoom was a rather wet and lonely Jack, and for the first time the wide grin was missing. I ordered two teas, and he handed me a pink charge sheet. I read it and realised that Jack had been driving while disqualified again.

'Oh, Jack,' I said in disbelief. 'How on earth could you get another charge while you're on bail? You know what this means.'

Jack shrugged, and nodded acceptance of the fate that was to befall him.

'What were you doing?' I asked him.

'About ninety-five miles an hour,' he said, attempting to revitalise the grin. 'I'd only gone to the chip shop when PC Cawley clocked me.'

PC Cawley had clocked him many times before, and on each occasion Jack had been charged with an offence. 'He must've seen me go into the chip shop and the cheating bastard hid, watched me get into the car, and then pulled me up at the bottom of our road. What a snide git he is.'

I found it difficult to sympathise with Jack, as the policeman was only doing his job and Jack had been warned not to do anything illegal while on bail. I was also distraught, because imprisonment was the likely sentence, so all the good work we had done in preparing his case was lost. How could the court sympathise with somebody who had gone out and committed the same crime yet again?

'I'm sorry I've let thee down,' Jack said.

'You haven't, Jack,' I replied. 'It's just that I don't want you to be sent to prison.'

'Don't worry, Steve,' he said. 'Tha'll do tha' best, and if I have to go to prison, well, I reckon I'll get my old job back in the bakery. But I'm a bit worried about Madge and the kids.'

Jack was an absolute delight to act for, because he was realistic, undemanding and, above all, in a funny kind of way a gentleman – a quality sadly lacking in some of the people appearing before court today. I'm afraid the old saying 'Honour amongst thieves' no longer exists, if indeed it ever did.

I was thinking about this when the emphysemic usher called us in. I was glad to get out of the tea-room, which was like the Grand Bazaar in Istanbul, with its smell of cigarette smoke and unwashed bodies.

In Court One, I found the Chairman of the Bench was Mr Norcliffe, an experienced magistrate who wasn't given to sympathy when he believed a defendant had been mocking the system. It was the worst Bench I could have got for Jack's case. In the courts you're always dealing with different personalities, and any one Bench may take a different view of a case from another. Mr Norcliffe had always been courteous to me, but he wasn't afraid to send people down, and consequently was no favourite of defence advocates. I was cursing my luck when Jack was called into court.

'What is your full name?' asked Mr Cook, the Clerk to the Justices.

'Jack Heptonstall, sir,' said Jack, in the most respectful tone he could muster.

'And your address and date of birth?' added Mr Cook.

Jack answered, using the word 'sir' at regular intervals. I looked at him and thought how smart he looked, in his dark blue suit, green shirt, red tie and pink pocket handkerchief. I had asked him to attend court dressed up, which in Yorkshire means wearing your best clothes. Jack was dressed up all right, but what as? The tie was so bright you needed dark glasses. It had an anchor on it, and being an old Navy man, Mr Norcliffe asked me which naval squadron it represented.

I said I wasn't sure, though I knew Jack had never been in the Navy. But Mr Norcliffe looked at his colleagues with a reassuring nod, confiding to them, 'Yes, Navy man.'

As Mr Cook started to put the charges, Norcliffe's eyebrows shot up his forehead and he glared piercingly at Jack. I looked at Jack to see if I could work out the object of concentration, and realised that his fly was undone.

Mr Norcliffe stopped the proceedings and had a *sotto voce* conversation with his clerk, who beckoned me over and whispered the problem in my ear. Jack remained blissfully unaware of anything untoward as I asked the court's leave to take further instructions from my client, then leaned across and whispered in his ear, 'Your flies are undone.'

Of course I *would* get Jack's deaf ear, and he asked me to repeat it. I then stood to conceal him from the Bench while he rectified the situation, only to have an embarrassed Jack report that the zip had broken. I suggested he take his jacket off and hold it in a suitable position in front of him. He didn't seem to favour the idea, but I insisted, and the general aura of the court seemed to force Jack to my will. But when he did so, I saw with horror that he had

15

only one sleeve on his shirt. He looked at me, shrugged, and said, 'It got tore, tha knows, dog pulled it off t'line…. When I pulled it, dog pulled back, and t'sleeve came off. It's a big dog, tha knows, strong jaws, it's a bad bastard really.'

The court clerk had had enough, and asked if we could get on with it. He read out the charges, and Jack pleaded guilty. I then found that he was serving a year's suspended sentence he'd forgotten to tell me about. That was the kiss of death as far as Mr Norcliffe was concerned, and Jack got two months' imprisonment, which was a fairly good result taking everything into account.

As they took Jack down the steel staircase to the cells, he winked at me and gave me a thumbs-up: when I saw him afterwards, he thanked me for my efforts and said he'd expected six months. We worked out his release date, which would only be some four to six weeks away, and he said he would look me up on his release and buy me a pint.

'So long as you don't bring Albert,' I said. 'Neither I nor my fish have recovered from his last visit.'

Jack laughed, the huge grin reappearing on his face, and as I left he was talking the warder into making him a cup of tea. Walking back up the staircase, I remembered the tie.

'Jack, there's something I forgot to ask. Let me have a look at your tie.'

He approached me, and I recognised a golden anchor. On closer scrutiny I saw three words printed around it: 'Captain Bird's Eye.'

'Where did you get it, Jack?' I asked.

'Tesco,' he replied proudly. 'Twenty-eight vouchers. Aw reet, i'nt it?'

My last case that day concerned a gipsy who was up for stealing electricity. Henry Fordham lived in a caravan pulled by a Transit van. He had been spotted down a dark lane by a police patrol, who were intrigued to see this caravan amongst a row of street lights which weren't working. The caravan itself was incredibly well lit, and a stereo was working full blast in it. They parked a short distance away and looked inside. Henry was sitting in front of a portable sun-tanning machine, in a yoga position, and his three children were busy playing Space Invaders.

It was clearly impossible to fuel those contraptions with a twelve-volt car battery, and when the police got round to the other side of the caravan they saw a cable reaching from beneath it to the street light. Henry had worked out how to use the street lighting system to power just about every working part of his caravan.

Henry's statement said it was the first time he had ever tried it (although the police's alternative explanation would certainly account for various areas of Sheffield regularly losing their street lights over a lengthy period). The magistrates adjourned for probation reports to be prepared, as they have to if they decide a case is too serious for a fine or conditional discharge, and are looking at a custody or community service sentence. Henry was released on bail, and neither I nor the court has seen him since. The last I heard, Nottingham was having difficulty with its street lights…

I returned to the office with mixed feelings about my day in court, and Anne told me that a lady called Madge was waiting to see me, with a boy who was trying to electrocute the fish in our tank. Madge was Jack's wife, who had been unable to find out which prison he had been sent to and wondered if I could help.

While I phoned the Allocation Centre, Albert watched me with his disconcerting grin. I avoided mentioning Jack's name so as not to upset him: I just said 'Hull' to Madge, and left it at that. But as they left, Albert turned to me and said, 'Hull Prison, eh? Piece of cake. Tarra for now, Steve.'

I shook my head. 'What is he going to be like?' I thought, and set about my dictation.

THREE

BODGER GOES FOR BUST AND THEN TRAGEDY COMES TO CALL

Wilford Smith had been in business for four months when Sheila, my secretary from my old firm, joined us, and we also employed a full-time receptionist called Tracy. Things were looking up, as I had a busy court diary and Wilford was doing well with conveyancing. In financial terms, I was probably better off then than at any other time in my career, because work was coming in and our overheads weren't excessive.

I had tremendous support from home. Jennifer knew how important it was for me to make a go of self-employment, and even helped out with secretarial duties at times. Dad, who was a brilliant painter, helped when he could, at weekends and after his own working day – I suppose you could say it was a bit of a family affair. That made life a lot easier for me, since necessity decreed I had to spend long hours working, a lot of them out of the office.

One lunchtime Wilford and I were in the Cross Keys when a friend called Tim Johnson, the manager of a local building society, joined us, and asked if we knew a builder who might be able to repair his office's security door, which was sticking. He needed somebody that afternoon, as the area manager was calling to inspect the branch, and Tim wanted everything in order for him.

'Broomy's your man,' said Wilford. 'He knows a bit about doors, he's cheap, and he'll be available. Give Bodger a ring.'

'Bodger?' queried Tim warily.

'Oh, yes,' said Wilford, realising that he had created a bit of an alarm, 'that's his nickname. It's a joke.'

'Leave it with us, Tim,' I said, seeing concern creep over his face. 'We'll get Bodg… Broomy on the job.'

We finished lunch and went back to the office, from where Wilford rang Bodger, telling him that a large security door needed to be repaired. 'Very good,' said Bodger, 'I'll bring my hammer.'

Within the hour Bodger was there with his toolbox – and his hammer – and Wilf introduced him to Tim. 'Ar' do?' said Bodger. 'Is tha aw reet?'

'Certainly,' said Tim, studying the man in front of him. Bodger was just under six foot tall and had a strong face with bright blue eyes that lit up when he laughed. He had a boxer's nose and ears that could have graced a professional wrestler, but unfortunately one of them didn't work properly, so you had to speak to him at his right side. He described himself as a 'tradesman', but I would have described him as a man with a hammer. Bodger and Tim shook hands, and Tim winced, such was the strength of Bodger's grip.

Tim explained the problem to Bodger, who became concerned when he realised that the door was made of aluminium. He stared at it, perplexed. 'Very difficult stuff to get nails into,' said Bodger.

Tim left him and disappeared into his office to work, his concentration disturbed by the sound of hammering from the front door. Four hours and six Anadins later there was a blessed silence, and he went outside to find the entire door and front window propped up in the street outside.

'What the fu-?' said Tim.

'Nice job, that,' said Bodger with great confidence. 'Don't worry, I'll have it back in a jiff and it'll fit perfick.'

It was 5pm and the area manager was due at 6.30pm, together with fifty or so visitors, all of whom were going to have the wares of the building society laid before them in the hope of attracting investment. Tim, seeing Bodger open a new box of nails, phoned Wilf in desperation. 'Does he know what he's doing?' he asked, with a tremor in his voice.

'Of course he does. He's always building something or other, isn't he?' said Wilf, looking at me imploringly.

I shook my head and lifted my tie as if hanging myself. Wilf made a rude gesture and returned to his reassurances.

'What time are you coming?' asked Tim.

'Six-thirty sharp,' said Wilf.

'I've got some Gevrey Chambertin '79,' said Tim invitingly.

'Six then,' said Wilf, and the call was over.

We set off at 5.45pm and walked the short distance down the road to Tim's office. As we approached, something glinted in the bright, early-evening sunshine. It was Bodger's mighty hammer, repeatedly connecting with the side of the door. A variety of nails lay at his feet, damaged beyond usefulness. I dared to look at the door and window frame, and they looked surprisingly good.

Bodger opened the door and closed it six or seven times to prove that this was a job well done.

'Excellent, Bodger,' I said approvingly. 'It works!'

''Course it works, you daft bugger,' said Bodger, indignant that I might have doubted him.

Tim was delighted. 'Please come in,' he said, 'and get to the buffet before anyone comes.' Bodger took four pieces of pork pie and ate ravenously, while Wilf concentrated on the wine.

Tim started to read the guest list, which began with His Worship the Mayor, a nice bloke in his late fifties with a considerable beer belly which made the top of his trousers curl over. We laughed when we saw that Sean Page had been invited: Sean has a lunatic sense of humour, especially when well-lubricated.

'He's been told to be on his best behaviour,' said Tim sternly. I looked at Wilf and Bodger. We knew that Pagey had been playing golf in a charity tournament, and the beer had been free.

At 6.30pm the area manager arrived – the archetypal area manager, down to the C&A suit and brogue shoes. His hair was suspiciously unlike the real thing, the colour on top not quite matching the sides, and the nape hanging at least an inch away from the back of his head.

'Eighty quid?' I ventured to Wilf.

'No more than that,' said Wilf knowledgeably.

The area manager, who smelt strongly of Aramis aftershave and garlic dip, surveyed the buffet and drinks table with the air of a sergeant major, then inspected his troops, resplendent in their society-issue frocks and jackets. More people arrived, including a chap called Victor from one of the local banks. He was less than average height, with bottle glasses which concealed a squint, and also smelt of Aramis with a hint of garlic dip. I introduced him to Bodger. 'Victor's a banker,' I shouted into Bodger's deaf ear.

'He looks aw reet to me. Don't worry, cock, Smithy's rude to everyone,' he told the confused Victor.

The area manager, Gerald McAndlish, was introduced to Bodger, who immediately noticed the toupee and stared at the man's head while they talked. 'Do you know many people here?' asked McAndlish, making polite conversation.

'One or two,' said Bodger. 'That's Wilford, and that's Smithy, and there's Fred the Mayor, I used to work with him at the foundry.'

'Who's that small chap with the bottle glasses?' Gerald asked.

'Beg pardon?' asked Bodger, caught on his deaf side. Gerald repeated his question. 'Don't know,' said Bodger, 'but Smithy says he's a bit of a wanker.' He then set off for a refill, leaving McAndlish completely perplexed.

I managed a word with Tim, who told me how impressed he was with Broomy's workmanship. 'I didn't think he'd manage it in time, but he's done very well. There was quite a gap between the door and the frame, it must have been at least an inch.'

At that point Broomy joined us, with another seven pieces of pork pie and four chicken legs. Tim said, 'I'm just telling Smithy how impressed I am with your workmanship. You seem to have cured the gap between the door and the frame?'

'Definite,' said Bodger confidently. 'You couldn't get a gnat's cock in that gap now.'

I was unable to contain a mouthful of Newcastle Brown, which went straight down the front of my shirt. As Broomy walked off, wondering what all the fuss was about, Tim said, 'He's got a way with words, hasn't he?'

The evening went very well until Pagey walked in.

Pagey stands out in a crowd. He is a little over six feet, with blond hair which at that time covered most of his head (he has now lost nearly all of it, he claims due to worry), and a round, jolly face with a perpetual infectious grin – for all the world Steerforth from *Great Expectations*, but with laughs. He was wearing golfing shoes, tartan trousers, an Yves St Laurent shirt with a golfing motif on the chest pocket and a Haldini silk cravat under an elegant cream jacket, and was puffing on a large Havana cigar. It was evident that Lord Page, as I sometimes called him, had had a good day. He hadn't won the tournament outright, but had won one of the subsidiary prizes.

By now Jarvis had appeared, and Page insisted on showing us his prize, which turned out to be an extremely large, plucked turkey. Pagey threw it at Jarvis, then embarked on a trip round the room, waving it at people and shouting 'Christmas is coming!'

Then he spied the area manager's wig. 'My God, that's a good one,' he said. He marched the turkey across to McAndlish, dropped its legs onto his shoulder and its head onto his neat cushioned dome. Pagey moved the feet up and down the man's collar, much to the delight of the assembled party.

McAndlish jumped, causing his toupee to slip to one side. 'Oh, it had to be you! You're a maniac, Pagey,' he said angrily.

'Hello, Godfrey old chap, how are you?' said Pagey, who had clearly forgotten Gerald's real name.

'Much better for seeing you, Pagey,' said Gerald, 'and by the way, you owe me twenty pounds.'

I was relieved to see that Gerald knew Pagey, and the fact that he'd managed to laugh about the incident endeared him to the guests. By the end of the night he had really entered into the swing of things, even trying to match Pagey gin for gin. Having experienced that contest myself, I knew it was a big mistake.

At the end of the evening, Gerald insisted on a grand opening of the new door. He ordered the remaining guests, which included Wilford, Jarvis, Bodger, Pagey and me, together with one or two members of staff, to stand outside while he declared the door open. Everyone was in good spirits and good spirits were in everyone.

Gerald officially declared the door open, and then slammed it shut. He had to skip smartly out of the way as it quivered, then rolled out of its frame, falling to the floor in front of him. The window followed, together with its frame.

'So much for the gnat's cock!' Gerald shouted at the top of his voice – just as his wife arrived, unseen by him, to pick him up…

I didn't stay for the repair job, but I'm told that it was dealt with extremely quickly, both to the door and to Gerald.

The following morning, I was getting ready to leave for court when Tracy asked me if I could see a lady on a matter of great urgency and delicacy. I was intrigued, but only had five minutes because I didn't want to be late for court.

The lady, who was called Lorraine, was tall, slim, and very smart, wearing a blue suit that fitted so well it could have been made to measure. Unfortunately, she was also agitated to the point of incoherence. When I showed her to a seat and asked what the problem was, all I could make out was that her husband was going to kill her and I had to do something.

I was conscious of the pressure of time, and Lorraine was clearly too frightened to make sense in a hurry. I told her I'd be finished at court by noon, and if she would come back and see me then, I'd try to resolve her difficulties.

She asked if she could wait in the office, because she had told her husband she was going to see a solicitor, and was worried he might be in town looking for her. She even gave me a description of him, and asked would I mind looking out of the window to see if he was outside, just like the scene in *The 39 Steps* when 'Miss Smith' seeks assistance from Richard Hannay. I'd never had a client take refuge in the office before, so I was a little disappointed when I could see no one like Lorraine's husband in the street. I left her with Tracy and headed for court.

I was thinking about her all morning, because she seemed so frightened, and when I got back at 11.45am, I arranged for tea and took her into my room to tease out her story.

It seemed Lorraine and her husband had been married for about a year, and she had met him only a month before that. John Wilson was a salesman with the firm she joined as a supervising cashier; they hit it off, and within a week were going out together. He was very attentive, phoning her in the morning and afternoon, and seeing her for lunch and straight after work. Within a fortnight she allowed him to stay at her flat, and only days later, he popped the question over a candlelit dinner at an expensive restaurant in Derbyshire.

'I agreed immediately, and we got a special licence and did it, even though my mother didn't approve. He seemed the best thing that had ever happened in my life. I have a little girl, Louise, by my first marriage, who was four at the time. John took to her straight away. It was the happiest time of my life and I was completely blinded by what I thought was my love for him,' Lorraine went on.

'When did it start going wrong?' I asked sympathetically.

'Everything was wonderful for about a month, until some girls from the office invited me on a birthday night out. John said he didn't want me to stay out late, which seemed reasonable, so I agreed to return fairly early. But I enjoyed myself, and stayed later than I meant. I got home a little after 2am, bringing a bottle of his favourite beer as a peace offering. But when I got inside and offered him the beer, he snatched if off me and threw it against the wall. It shattered, and I just looked at him – I didn't know what to do, I was shocked. Then he seemed to lose control. He slapped my face, punched me, kicked me, and it woke Louise, who came downstairs and saw it, and started screaming. Eventually he stopped, and after a while I managed to get to my feet, pick Louise up, and lock us in the bathroom. We stayed there until the house was quiet, then crept into Louise's room, where I rocked her to sleep, curled up on her tiny bed.

'The next day, as soon as I heard him leave for work, I rang my mother and told her what had happened. She was extremely upset, and insisted that I go home. But before I could leave, John came back, carrying a bunch of roses. I didn't want to speak to him, but he started to cry and told me he'd imagined all sorts of things I might have been doing, and just flipped.'

'What did you do then?' I asked.

'I stayed with him,' said Lorraine, embarrassedly, 'and things were better for about another month, then it started up again. I got sick of the constant beatings, and said I wanted to leave him, but he told me that if I did he'd hurt Louise, and I believed him. For the rest of our time together I lived in fear and misery. I didn't dare leave the house for fear of what he might do, so I gave up my job, and then of course I was dependent on him for a living. I just didn't know which way to turn.

'Sometimes he tried to be nice, but I was always worried about Louise, and myself. I hid it from my mother because I didn't want to upset her, but one day when Louise was at her house Mum got her to explain what was wrong. She said Louise shouted, "He hit my mummy, he hit my mummy," over and over again. Well, I'd put up with him to protect Louise, but obviously she was being badly affected anyway, and I couldn't have that. I steeled myself, and told him again that I was going to leave.

'Next day, when I went to collect Louise from school, she wasn't there: a teacher said her stepfather had collected her. I panicked and called the police, who just advised me to wait. It wasn't until 9pm that John wandered in with Louise, claiming that they'd only been to the fair, and apologising for forgetting to tell me, but his smirk told me he'd done it on purpose. When he went to work the next day, I packed as many of our belongings as I could and we left. We're staying with a friend so as not to disturb Mum.'

She was transparently truthful, and I feared for her safety. I completed the forms to apply for an injunction (restraining one party from interfering with another), and a legal aid application, contacted the court for the earliest possible date, and managed to fix a hearing for the next morning. Lorraine agreed to be at the office at 9pm, where I would meet her and take her to court. I gave her a copy of the proposed injunction, with power of arrest, and she said enthusiastically, 'Louise and I'll be safe now.'

Lorraine again asked me to check the street and, looking out of the window, I was astonished to see a man lurking in a doorway, staring up at our rooms. From her description, it was her husband. He was a small man, some five feet five inches tall, with an unremarkable face, clean-shaven and smartly dressed in a dark suit. I held back a corner of the curtain, and Lorraine drew her breath in panic as she recognised him. Having heard her story I felt tempted to go out and give him a clout, but instead we got her out through the back door before he was any the wiser.

*

The next morning I waited on the office steps for Lorraine. When at 9.50 she still hadn't arrived I began to worry, as the court hearing had been arranged for 10.30. I went back into the office and rang the two telephone numbers she'd given me, but there was no answer.

Just after 10 o'clock Tracy told me there were two policemen to see me. It was extremely inconvenient, because I'd have to rush to court to try to explain why Lorraine was late, but I called them in. Both officers were grim-faced.

'Not guilty,' I said, trying to lighten the proceedings, but it was clear that neither was in the mood for merriment. 'What's wrong?' I asked.

The sergeant said, 'I understand that you were representing Lorraine Wilson.'

'Yes,' I said. 'I'm with her in court this morning, but she's not turned up yet…' Then I cottoned on. 'What do you mean, *were*?'

'I'm afraid she's not going to turn up,' said the sergeant. 'At about 6pm last night, Mrs Wilson was walking to the bus station when her husband approached her. Witnesses say that she refused to speak to him and turned away, but he took a knife from his pocket and stabbed her several times. One of the blows pierced the heart, and she died almost immediately.'

I sank into my chair in disbelief. 'Have you got him?' I asked.

The sergeant said that Wilson had told a witness that when the police came he'd be in the pub across the road. Within minutes they were on the scene, and he was arrested. It seems he sat quite calmly in the pub, drinking a glass of whisky.

'He told us he meant to kill her, and he's before the magistrates this morning on a murder charge. At least eight people witnessed it, and he never tried to get away. It's one of the most cold-blooded murders I've ever been involved with,' said the sergeant despondently.

Apparently Lorraine had had her copy of my proposed injunction in her hand, which was how they knew I was acting for her, and they asked if I would make a statement for the record to prove that we'd applied for it. We agreed I could make it that afternoon, and I set off for court in a daze.

I didn't spend much time in the County Court, so wasn't used to fastening the wing collar's brass studs, and was still trying to do so when my case was called. Dashing into the courtroom just as His Honour Judge Walker came into court, I explained to him what had happened.

When I finished, the judge said, 'The case will be marked withdrawn.' I bowed and turned to leave, the Clerk of the Court called the next case, and that was that. Lorraine Wilson was just another statistic.

Six months later, Wilson appeared at Sheffield Crown Court pleading not guilty to murder but guilty to manslaughter. The jury found him guilty of murder, and he was sentenced to life imprisonment. He remains in prison to this day.

A week after that, a lady with a little girl aged about five came to the office. 'I'm Lorraine's mother,' said the lady. 'Could you please spare me a few minutes?'

'Of course,' I said. 'Louise will be all right here with Tracy: come into my office.'

I offered her tea, which she refused, and asked Tracy to give Louise a pen and some paper to pass the time.

Mrs Yardley told me that Wilson had written to her demanding to see the child, and she wanted to know what she could do. She gave me his letter, which was politely written, but ended with the words, 'Louise is the only connection I have left with Lorraine.'

Appalled, I told her that no court would accede to such a request, and offered to write to Wilson myself, which put her mind at rest. I dictated the letter in front of her, and it merely said,

Dear Sir,

RE: Louise

Your letter has been passed to me. I write to inform you that your request is refused. There will be no replies made to any further communications.

Yours faithfully,

I asked about Louise, and was told that she had settled down well after a very difficult start. 'Young children forget,' said Mrs Yardley authoritatively. 'Fortunately, she hasn't been scarred!'

When I ushered her out to reception, Louise went straight to her and took her hand. I watched them walk downstairs, the little girl clinging to her grandmother, pausing only to wave to me as she moved out of sight. I went back into the waiting room, and couldn't help noticing a child's drawing on the coffee table. It was of a woman in a blue suit, with 'Mummy' written underneath.

FOUR

CORGI 1 – YOBS 0

One warm August day, I went into the toilet to change into my football gear. Avoiding the ballcock, I put on the blue-and-white hooped shirt, but found I had only one sock; I'd have to borrow one from Lidster when I got to the ground. We were playing a large firm of solicitors from Sheffield, a very good team, but were confident because we had the Lidster brothers.

It started to rain as I drove across town, but was still warm, and the rain would be refreshing during the match. A worse blow was that David Lidster, one of the mainstays of the squad, told us his big toe was going septic, so tonight he would have to play in defence. I played as a striker, but lacked fitness: I could contribute the odd goal when the wind was in the right direction, providing I wasn't expected to run about too much. Our weakest link was our reserve goalkeeper; only the first-choice goalie had two legs.

By the time the game got under way the rain was pouring down, but within a quarter of an hour I was sweating profusely. By half-time we were leading 1–0 but beginning to tire, and the opposition had more reserves of energy to call upon. What's more, Dave Lidster had been injured, and removed his right boot to display the most offensive-looking big toe I've ever seen, twice its normal size and clearly septic. I asked him what had happened and he said he'd hurt it kicking the opposition's centre forward 'up the arse'. The match ended at 4–4, with Lidster in goal and our one-legged reserve keeper standing to his right, blocking half the goalmouth with his considerable bulk.

In the pub after the match, Dave again exhibited his foot, and as he pressed it, yellow pus shot out. The other players, particularly the ones eating sandwiches, bellowed displeasure, and I said, 'You're going to have serious trouble with that foot, Dave, if you don't have it seen to. You want to be careful. Douglas Bader started with sepsis, and look what happened to him.'

Dave thought for a minute and then announced, with his unique brand of logic: 'But Bader didn't have any legs!'

At least six of the eleven players present spat out their beer, overtaken by laughter. Dave amused us even more when he asked what we were laughing at. From then on, Dave Lidster became Bader.

When I arrived at the office the following morning an old lady, accompanied by a small corgi, was waiting to see me, nervously twisting the dog lead in her fingers. She wore an elderly but still-smart green tweed suit, and her hair must have been done specially for this visit. She said her name was Mary Daniels, and she had called to see me without an appointment in the hope that I would give her some urgent advice. She had the air of a lady with a lot on her mind, but I was extremely surprised when she showed me a criminal summons for assault.

I invited her into the office and offered tea, which she politely declined, as she wished to talk about her problem without further ado. She handed me a neatly folded bail sheet, which gave the date and time of her court hearing.

Mrs Daniels told me she was seventy-three and a widow, her husband having died of cancer some ten years before. She had no children or close relatives, and lived in a maisonette on the outskirts of Rotherham, having sold the matrimonial home because it held too many memories for her. Her only company, apart from her weekly visit to an old friend in a retirement home, was her corgi, Dancer, on whom she obviously doted.

Her eyes narrowed as she related the facts of her case. For some time a gang of youths had been congregating near her home, terrorising the local pensioners by throwing eggs and old fish-and-chip containers at them. But Mrs Daniels was of the old school, and believed she should be able to speak to young people without fear. She had complained to these yobs on occasions when out walking her dog, but was always met with abuse.

Unfortunately, the yobs had 'marked her card', and were delighted to see her on the night in question. They surrounded her, throwing eggs and then taunting and abusing her. Dancer understandably took exception to his owner being threatened like this, so he barked and pulled at the lead. One of the yobs kicked the dog, and Dancer yelped in pain. Mrs Daniels, fearing for the dog's safety, struck out with a spare lead she carried in her other hand, to allow the dog to walk on a longer lead, then scurried away to safety. She said she hadn't really thought what might happen, but the buckle had apparently caught the young man in the eye, causing a serious injury. The police were called, a complaint was taken, and a CID officer had the unenviable task of calling to ask Mrs Daniels to accompany him to the police station. She told me neither she nor her husband had ever been involved in any form of trouble, but, although she clearly felt upset at having to appear in court, she kept her dignity throughout.

As she told me her story, I felt angry at the way she'd been treated. She had managed to get to the age of seventy-three without a stain on her character, and now, in her twilight years, was being forced into this humiliation. To be fair, it wasn't the police's fault – if someone had suffered a serious injury, they had to take action. (The system has now changed, with the Crown Prosecution Service reviewing all cases, and I'd be astonished if she were prosecuted today.) I was so moved by her plight that the question of money never entered my head. She reminded me of it by saying that she had some savings and her widow's pension, and could pay for representation: she even wanted to pay something on account, but I said we'd worry about it later.

I again offered her tea, and this time she accepted. I asked Annie to bring it in the china cups we'd bought for VIP guests. (We only had four left, because the handle had come off one during washing and Albert had broken the other.) Mrs Daniels trembled as she held hers, the saucer rattling against it in tune with her nerves. But I was delighted when she told me that I'd put her mind at rest on a number of points, and would look forward to seeing me at court on the first appearance date.

On the appointed morning, I waited outside the court for my client. The courthouse was dilapidated, with few facilities, no air-conditioning, and a large population of ne'er-do-wells, some quite intimidating, hanging about the court corridor and anterooms and hawking dodgy goods. Determined not to subject Mrs Daniels to that, I took her straight into the courtroom, away from prying eyes and the 'Rolex' salesmen. After a consultation with a helpful clerk, I called her case first, and a not guilty plea was entered to the charge. As she stood in the dock giving her plea, one of the solicitors on the front bench next to me asked me what she was in for. When I answered assault, he looked incredulous and exclaimed 'Never!'

The clerk went through the formalities, asking Mrs Daniels her date of birth. She gave it and said, 'And I am seventy-three years of age.' It wasn't a protest or a complaint: it was simply an old lady who thought the court would want to know.

The Chairman of the Magistrates was polite to her, and released her on bail. But as we left the court, two youths pushed past us in their haste to get in. I remonstrated, and one of them looked at me with a blank expression and said, 'Tha what?'

'Never mind, you wouldn't understand what manners are anyway,' I muttered.

'Eh?' came the reply. I thought I might phone the Natural

History Museum and tell them that Neanderthal man was alive and well and living in Rotherham.

That evening I wrote to the prosecution suggesting they drop the proceedings. They replied that the complainant and his family had been to their local councillor and MP, insisting that the prosecution continue, so it would have to go to court.

On the morning of the case, Mrs Daniels was extremely nervous and suffering from stress-induced breathlessness, so I took her to an interview room and bought her a cup of tea from the WRVS kiosk. Her tea remained untouched as we rehearsed what would happen during the trial. As we waited, I noticed a group of four or five youths sitting towards the end of the corridor, who were clearly the prosecution witnesses. On the pretext of going into the solicitors' room, I walked past them to see what I was up against. They were all wearing white shirts and smart ties – their parents had done their bit to ensure their children were as presentable as possible – and when I heard a middle-aged couple standing with the youths mention something about compensation, I realised the real reason behind the charade of the court case.

The prosecutor, a pleasant chap, told me he was as unhappy as me about prosecuting the case, but there was nothing he could do about it, and even the hard-bitten clerk of the court obviously sympathised with my client. The bench were called in, three magistrates in all, two of them elderly, which I thought was an advantage to me. The third was a lady in her forties, so there was a chance her parents would be in the same age-group as Mrs Daniels.

My colleague opened up his papers and produced some colour photographs, which showed a nasty injury to the lad's eye. The clerk called Mrs Daniels forward and she answered her name, address and date of birth, giving her age again, and pleaded not guilty. I could see the bench weighing her up, as they had no prior information about the case. (In the Crown Court judges usually have the papers served on them beforehand, but this isn't possible in the magistrates' court because of the number of cases.)

The prosecutor rose and outlined his case, which was that on the night in question a group of five lads were on their way home when they met the defendant. One claimed that he had tried to stroke the dog, which snapped at him, so he accused the lady of owning a vicious dog. The prosecutor told the court that, without justification, Mrs Daniels lost her temper and struck out at the lad with her spare lead, catching him in the eye and causing serious injury.

The complainant was then called to the witness box. He left out any reference to throwing eggs at the old lady, or dancing round her shouting obscenities, and as he passed Mrs Daniels he sneered at her. The magistrates saw it, and I knew we'd got off to a good start.

When the prosecutor had taken him through his story, he asked the youth if he had done anything to cause the lady to act as she had. Much to my surprise, he didn't answer straight away, but eventually said, 'Not really'. Fearing to open a can of worms, the prosecutor didn't pursue that, but sat down and stared at me, raising his eyebrows.

I got to my feet, stared at the youth, and waited until he dropped his gaze. 'What do you mean, not really?' I asked forcefully.

He hesitated, then said, 'I didn't do anything to cause it.'

'Who threw the egg at her?' I demanded.

'Not me,' said the lad.

'So someone did throw an egg?' I continued.

'Well, yes,' said the lad.

'Why didn't you mention the egg when you first gave your story to the prosecutor?' I asked.

There was no reply, and the youth buried his chin into his chest. I waited a long time, knowing I wouldn't get an answer, but hoping the silence would highlight his reluctance to say anything.

Then I asked, 'Why did you all laugh when the egg hit her?'

The youth clearly thought I knew what had happened, and seemed frightened of being shown up as a liar. He began to back-pedal, but I pressed on, asking who had thrown the egg and who had laughed. Eventually I said, 'For the last time, did you laugh?'

I couldn't believe my luck when he replied that he had. My next question was obvious. 'Because it was funny?'

He had no option but to answer, 'Yes.'

'If I threw an egg at your grandmother, would you find it funny?'

The lad's head sank deeper into his chest as he said, 'Dunno.' I seized my opportunity and threw a barrage of questions at him, and eventually got him to agree that the whole group had laughed. Then I asked who'd kicked the dog.

''Tweren't me,' he answered, clearly accepting that someone had. He was a pathetic witness, and his parents' interruptions from the back of the court didn't help him.

The next witness came in, and gave exactly the same account as the complainant. I began my cross-examination as before, asking who had thrown the egg at the old lady. This youth, a cocky clever-dick, completely denied that any egg had been thrown or the dog kicked.

I asked him if his friend, the complainant, was the sort of lad who could be believed, and he said that he was. I asked him if the egg incident and the kicking of the dog could have happened with-out him seeing them. (Fortunately the clerk didn't stop this unfair question.) The witness was adamant neither ever took place, and if it had he would have seen.

I paused for what seemed an eternity before I spoke.

'Your friend just agreed that an egg was thrown and the dog was kicked. Therefore I put it to you, young man, that you're telling lies.'

'Well yes, er no, er, I don't know,' he shouted.

The magistrates began to whisper to each other, clearly unhappy about the way things were going. I leaned across to ask the prosecutor if he was going to continue. He said he'd call another witness, and a third youth took the stand. (Witnesses can only remain in court after they have given evidence, so they can't hear what earlier witnesses have said.)

Another cocky youth with a sneer told exactly the same tale as the other two. I therefore followed the same line of attack.

'Who threw the egg?'

'Not me,' came the reply.

'So an egg was thrown, then?' I asked.

'Not that I saw,' came the reply.

'So why did you say it wasn't you?'

'You got me all confused,' he said.

'But it was the first question I asked you, how could you be confused about that?' I asked. I then took a risk, for Mrs Daniels had told me that this was the one that had kicked the dog. I asked, 'Why did you kick the dog?'

'Because it bit me,' he said.

This lad was now telling a different story from his mates. To my surprise, he admitted that an egg was thrown, the dog was kicked, and the whole group had laughed.

'The old lady struck out with a lead to frighten you off, didn't she?' I asked. 'I suggest that she was frightened for herself and her dog, so she struck out with the lead at a group of five lads who had surrounded her. If you'd been surrounded like that, and had an egg thrown at you, would you have been frightened?'

'I s'pose,' he replied. 'But we were only larking about.'

With that I sat down. The prosecutor buried his head in his hands, and I asked the court to consider a submission of no case (the procedure when the prosecution case is so bad it should be stopped there and then).

The magistrates retired very briefly, and returned to say the case would be dismissed. The father of the complainant swore, and was ordered out of the courtroom. I applied for Mrs Daniels' costs to be paid out of central funds, which meant she wouldn't have to pay her solicitor's fees, and the court agreed. As we left the court one of the yobs shouted, 'We'll get you for this, you old cow!' I felt sorely tempted to go across and belt him around the ear, but thought better of it.

Mrs Daniels, showing emotion for the first time since I'd met her, began to cry with relief. She shook my hand warmly, but it was some minutes before she was able to pull herself together. As she set off down the road she paused to turn, smile and wave. I shouted, 'Corgis 1, Yobs Nil!', and she laughed. This was one occasion I was convinced that justice had been done.

On my way out of the office the following day I noticed that a parcel had been left for me in reception. It was a chocolate cream cake Mrs Daniels had made, with a card which read, 'Thank you, I will never forget you.'

I never saw her again, but I heard from the police that a group of yobs had smashed all her windows, and the council were seeking to rehouse her. I discovered that the only place she could go was a council flat where pets weren't allowed, and I desperately wanted to help her, but she didn't call. I wrote to her old address, but the letter was returned marked 'gone away', and when I checked at the council offices they said she had left the area without a forwarding address.

A year later, on the anniversary of the acquittal, a box holding a chocolate cream cake arrived in reception, with a card which read, 'To Mr Smith, with grateful thanks for all you did for me a year ago. I will never forget you, with very best wishes, Mrs Daniels.' For the next three years I received a chocolate cream cake, boxed with a card, but sadly on the fifth anniversary no cake arrived.

FIVE

IRISH JOKES, SICK NOTES AND MEDICALS

It was a beautiful summer in 1981, and Wilford and I were very happy with the way that business was going. On the litigation side, I was frantically busy, and had to work hard to get round all my court appointments, see the clients and keep the paperwork to manageable levels. Jennifer remained supportive, bearing the brunt of domestic arrangements and looking after our daughter, as well as doing some secretarial work. Rebecca was doing well at school, and showing an aptitude for singing and drama – I took the Saturday morning off to attend her first music festival, and tried not to show how thrilled I was when she won it outright. Obviously she too had caught the showbusiness bug!

Life wasn't without its difficulties, and the main ones for solicitors are the clients, without whom the job would be quite enjoyable. The bigger the trouble they're in, the bigger the problem for us. Some clients are incredibly devious, and the clever ones are the worst. The modern tendency towards negligence actions protects the vulnerable but gives a forged licence to the dishonest, and it never ceases to surprise me just how devious some people can be – necessity is the mother of invention, and I've certainly represented some real inventors in my time. This is never more apparent than when criminals decide they don't want to attend their own trials.

Most defendants dislike attending court, and will use any excuse to put off the evil day. In thirty years in the profession I have seen the full songbook of excuses for failing to turn up, of which the sick note is a perennial favourite – it's always been a source of wonder to me how defendants manage to get them. They seem to be able to simulate all manner of illnesses, and some even write out their own notes; one committed a burglary at a doctor's surgery just to steal a prescription pad and a wad of sick notes. My perennial client Jack Heptonstall once turned up with a sick note describing his condition as 'tired and listless'. The court were not impressed, and issued a warrant for his arrest. Another client sent a sick note with the ailment described as 'rash to feet (both)'; the magistrates didn't accept that either.

The list is endless, but one of my favourites had to be Seamus, an Irishman with red curly hair and very pale skin. He had visited one of the large stores in Sheffield and used the store's own credit card with a limit of £400, which is supplied to valued customers. Seamus decided to buy items to almost that value, so he picked out a toaster and a mini hi-fi, and handed over his credit card. The girl looked at it and immediately suggested that she might wrap the items so they'd be easier to carry. Seamus thanked her, and said he'd look around the store for five minutes while she did so.

However, the shop assistant went straight to the telephone and called the police. When Seamus came to pick up his ill-gotten gifts, he felt a hand on his shoulder, and the words, 'You're under arrest for handling a stolen credit card,' rang in his ears.

Seamus, baffled by the store's apparent omniscience, asked the burly police sergeant how they'd got him. 'The name on the card is Tariq Mahmood Hussain. You don't look like a Tariq Mahmood Hussain to me,' said the sergeant.

This wasn't the first time Seamus had been involved in dishonesty, as only five months before he had been given a suspended sentence for deception. He knew, therefore, that prison was inevitable, and he simply couldn't face it. I appeared at Sheffield magistrates' court to represent him, and of course he failed to show. A sick note was handed to the magistrates, which had a word scribbled out and written underneath in red biro 'very ill'. Unfortunately my Irish friend had signed it with his own name, S. Monoghan. He was eventually arrested and sentenced to nine months' imprisonment. The last I heard of him, he'd gone back to Ireland to work on a farm. He certainly wasn't suited to city life!

Doctors' handwriting is a standard joke, but I don't believe they're any better or worse than the rest of us – though I do remember one sick note I couldn't read at all. I handed to the chairman of the magistrates to see if he could decipher it, and he announced boldly that it appeared to read 'brown shorts'. We never did find out exactly what that problem was.

I also remember handing a court clerk a certificate which bore the word 'scabies', a highly contagious condition involving a mite which burrows under the skin, causing skin eruptions and dreadful irritation; you can usually tell a sufferer by the way that he persistently scratches. This particular clerk of the court, who was in a bad mood, advised the magistrates that such a condition shouldn't preclude anyone from attending court, and invited them to issue a warrant for the defendant's arrest. Since he'd been quite rude to me, I took pleasure in explaining that the condition was highly contagious, and could even be passed on from items that had been in the defendant's possession. The clerk dropped the sick note in horror onto his desk, much to the amusement of the other solicitors.

Apart from the question of sick notes, I've always had an interest in health and alternative medicine. My job was extremely stressful, with punishing schedules, rushed and indeed missed meals – this regularly exasperated Jennifer, who spent many evenings waiting to serve a meal courtesy of the microwave. (Her friends often asked how she put up with me, but in her usual protective manner she told them that I paid the mortgage!). So I resolved to try to do something about it.

The Great Jarvis is fairly healthy apart from his liver (he had had a nasty scare about a year or so before, when his liver fell out with him, the medical term being cirrhosis, and he was told to abstain from alcohol for up to six months, and placed on a special diet), but as we were both well past the magic thirty, we decided to have a comprehensive medical check to establish that we were still alive. We chose a well-known private hospital in Leeds, were told to set a full morning aside, and agreed to treat ourselves afterwards to a large meal with plenty of grog, either to celebrate a clean bill of health or to commiserate if there was anything wrong. (We had been told not to eat or drink anything from teatime the previous day to ensure that our systems were clear, so that blood and urine samples would be easier to analyse.)

At the hospital a pleasant, self-assured, middle-aged lady escorted us to our lockers and supplied us with dressing-gowns. She explained that there were a male and a female doctor, the man elderly and, as she put it, 'All right apart from being deaf', the lady in her early 30s. I must confess that this worried me, because part of the examination was to test for hernias and things like that, which meant the old hands-down-the-shorts and engage-in-a-coughing-fit-while-your-tackle's-squeezed, and when the nurse had gone, Jarvis confessed that he too was embarrassed by female doctors. However, I was called by a smart man wearing horn-rimmed spectacles and the traditional white coat. I guessed he was about sixty, and he had Stewart Granger-style hair, brilliantly groomed, an expensive Italian silk tie, and a tailored shirt.

The tests passed without incident, until the rubber glove moment arrived. When you hear the doctor pull on a glove and say the magic words, 'Lie on your side and lift up your knees,' you know you're in for the dreaded internal.

I politely declined, saying that I felt perfectly well in that area, but mischievously added that my friend Mr Jarvis had been worried about difficulties there, but was too nervous to ask for the test.

My doctor said he would pass on the information to the person doing Jarvis's medical. From this I realised that Jarvis had got the female doctor, and I had to smile, knowing he was going to get the rubber-glove treatment from her!

Sure enough, Jarvis reappeared from his examination with a red face etched with horror. 'Do you know what she's just done to me?' he asked.

I couldn't contain my laughter, hearing only the words 'rubber glove' and 'my arse' from the tangled rhetoric.

To conclude the tests we were given an ECG, and much to my surprise, apart from being told I was overweight, I got a clean bill of health. Jarvis, however, was called back to the doctor's office, from where I could just hear him being asked to confirm his drinking habits, and Jarvis saying that he only had the occasional drink. 'Yes, occasionally in the morning, the afternoon, the evening and at night, lying bastard,' I thought to myself, as he reappeared with a relatively clean bill of health and some cream for the rubber burns.

'Did you get the rubber glove?' asked Jarvis, over a fine lunch at a local restaurant.

'No,' I said, faking shocked surprise.

'Well I can't understand why she did it to me, then,' said Jarvis.

'Perhaps she's particularly conscientious. Or just likes to do the rubber-glove treatment,' I suggested.

'I suppose you'll be telling the lads about this?' said Jarvis gloomily.

'Who, me?' I replied, the picture of innocence.

'Well at least we've got a clean bill of health,' he consoled himself.

'Yes,' I said. 'I'm pleased to hear your bowels are all right.'

He gave me a critical stare, beginning to realise that he'd been had. It took the rest of the meal and a good deal of grog to get him to see the funny side.

SIX

AN OAP GETS RIPPED OFF, SO THEY TRY TO TAKE HIS HOUSE

The best advice I can ever give any would-be litigant is, 'Don't do it.' It's a risky business that should be avoided at all costs, but of course sometimes people have no alternative, and it's my firm belief that judges do their best to be fair and produce the right results. This isn't always possible, and inevitably people sometimes leave the courts feeling disappointed. But if you do your best, at least your client won't be disappointed with *you*, so you'll live to fight another day.

One of my legal friends is Les Walton, a grammar-school boy with a high intellect, and a real character, with whom I had worked at my first firm in Barnsley, and who in the early 80s was a partner of a prestigious firm in Yeovil. In late 1981 Leslie made one of his flying visits north to kill a number of birds with one stone, including seeing my office for the first time.

I proudly showed him around, then, as we were enjoying a drink by the window of my office, we saw an old man in the street, busily sorting some papers and putting them into an envelope.

'It looks as though he's got something for you,' said Walton.

Sure enough, the old man shuffled to our front door, and we heard the papers fall to the floor with a thud, just as we heard the hoot from the taxi I'd ordered to take us to Jim Lidster's hotel-restaurant, the Brentwood in Rotherham (now under new management).

I picked up the envelope as we left and opened it in the taxi, to find a shakily written letter from one Eric Sharpe, who had got a mortgage with a loan company and apparently been unable to pay the instalments. The company had applied for an order for possession, which meant they wanted to kick him out of his home and sell it, using the proceeds to recover their dues. The summons showed that he had borrowed £13,000, repayable by fairly substantial instalments at an astonishingly high rate of interest. From his enclosures I saw that Mr Sharpe had signed the loan agreement, saying that he accepted and understood the terms, but the tenor of his letter gave me the impression that he was quite bewildered. Intrigued, I showed Walton the papers, and we decided it needed investigation.

At the Brentwood, we were greeted by James and his wife Angie. As James is a connoisseur of wines and Angie an expert in the kitchen, all we had to do was to sit there and consume, at which Walton and I are experts. The evening went extremely well, and when we left the hotel after midnight I felt wonderful.

I don't know what it is about good food, good wine and good company, but they seem to lose a lot of their attraction the next morning. However, I dictated a letter to Mr Sharpe offering him an appointment before setting off for court, feeling a little less than my best.

I finished court at about 12.30pm and had to be in the Huddersfield Magistrates' Court at two, so I took the short cut through the cells, where the prisoners were eating bangers, beans and mash. One of them shouted a request for more bread and the jailer, who had seen and heard it all, replied, 'Certainly sir, would that be white, brown, wholemeal or pikelet?'

'Fucking bread's what I asked for, fucking bread's what I want!'

'You can't have any fucking bread, there's no fucking bread left in this fucking cell area, for fucking you or any-fucking-one else. You can have a fucking biscuit if you want, otherwise fuck off.' As the jailer let me out and locked the door behind me, I heard him say, 'He's off the pudding list.' Dashing off to the car park, I couldn't help wondering why I had spent so many years taking difficult examinations and working as an articled clerk for next to nothing to qualify as a solicitor. Perhaps it was the charming after-dinner banter in the cell area I found so attractive.

When I got back from Huddersfield, I found I had two appointments. One was a lady who hadn't paid some fines and was frightened about going to prison, and the other was Eric Sharpe, who had made an appointment before he got my letter.

Eric Sharpe was 79, and a widower for twenty years. He'd been a self-employed market trader until he was 75, when he suffered a slight stroke, which left him partly paralysed down his right side, and with some mental impairment, so his mind didn't function as well as it had before. He shuffled into my room, head bowed, wearing an old but smart suit, slightly frayed at the cuffs, and a dark kipper tie, which he had clearly owned for a long time. His expensive shoes were rather worn, but he looked like a man who had known wealth, though his face was heavily lined, his eyes tired and bloodshot, and his snowy hair unkempt. He lowered himself into the leather armchair with a groan. We exchanged pleasantries briefly, then he began his story.

After his stroke he became acquainted with Linda Sharpe (no relation), who used to visit the patient in the next bed to Eric in the hospital, and over a three-month period they became friends.

'I thought she was a good girl,' he said. 'When she turned up at my house one day after I was released from hospital, saying that she'd just called as she was in the area, I was glad – I don't get too many visitors. I invited her for tea at the weekend, and after that Linda came to tea every week, usually on a Sunday.

'One Sunday she broke down in tears and told me she'd gone into business with a man she'd had an affair with, put all her money into it. But it failed, and he ran off, leaving her in debt. What's more, it turned out he hadn't been paying the rent, so she'd been evicted. Before I realised it, I'd told her she could stay with me while she sorted something out.

'The next day, she moved into the spare room. She couldn't pay any rent, because she had no money and couldn't claim benefits because she hadn't enough stamps on her card, so we agreed she'd be my temporary housekeeper, with free bed and board. We went on like this for six or eight months; she was good company, and my meals were always ready on time. I wasn't too well, and knew if she left I wouldn't be able to cope and might end up in a home, which I didn't want, because I've always enjoyed my independence. So I asked Linda if she'd stay permanently.

'But she was concerned about her own security. I have a daughter I rarely see, who'd inherit the house. But when I offered to put Linda into my will, she said my daughter might challenge it and she'd still end up homeless.'

'That's not true, Mr Sharpe. Your daughter could only challenge such a will if she was financially dependent upon you at the time of your death. Was she?' I asked.

'No,' said Mr Sharpe. 'She has her own business, and a far better income than me. Anyway, Linda said there was no need for that; she wanted to stand on her own two feet. Instead, she suggested I put some money into a business she wanted to start, as a mobile hairdresser: that way she could maintain her dignity and look after me at the same time. But I haven't a lot in the bank; my only asset was my bungalow. She told me not to worry about it, and we let it rest.'

Eric, who was quite obviously heartbroken, took a sip of tea to gather his composure, and his eyes hardened as he continued his story.

'One day she came in to say she had the chance to buy a van fitted with hairdressing equipment. She'd need £13,000, but she'd worked out a business plan, showing what her weekly earnings would be, and it looked good to me. She said she'd arrange a loan and make all the repayments out of her profits, and I would merely act as guarantor.'

'Did you realise what you were getting into?' I asked sympathetically.

'Not really, I wasn't too well at the time. But Linda seemed to know what she was doing, and one day a man from a loan company came to the house. He produced a lot of papers, and I thought we ought to get a solicitor to check them, but Linda told me she'd seen one, and he'd said they were all in order.

'I remember the day fairly well, because I was in a lot of pain and really wanted to go to sleep, and I was embarrassed at having this man I'd never met before in my bedroom. I signed the documents, about five of them.'

'Did you receive any acknowledgement through the post?'

'If I did, Linda dealt with it.'

'What happened then?' I asked.

'One Friday Linda said that she was going to visit a friend over the weekend – she'd bought the van by then. She never came back, or wrote or phoned. I was quite desperate, because I didn't know what had happened to her. Then one morning I was woken by the postman with a letter that required a signature. It was a final demand from the loan company, who said that only one payment had been received.

'I was horrified, because I'd never owed anyone anything, and I simply didn't know what to do. Then Linda telephoned, saying her friend had been taken ill and she'd been looking after her. I told her about the letter, but she said not to worry, she'd sort it out when she returned the following week. I don't know why I believed her, but I did, and simply threw the letter onto the fire.

'The next thing, I received all these papers about arrears and failing to pay and court costs, and a lady at the Age Concern place told me you might be able to help. I'm so worried, I don't know what to do. Will they take my house off me, Mr Smith?'

I felt truly sorry for this man, robbed of his health and his money and now facing losing his home. I gave him what reassurances I could, and told him I'd speak to the courts and adjourn the case if possible, to apply for legal aid and try to save his home.

The difficulty was that he had signed all the papers, in particular the loan agreement, which confirmed that he knew and understood the transaction. But as I looked at the documentation, I saw that his writing was that of a feeble old man: his signature looked as though it had been written in a moving vehicle. Except for one signature. On the photostat copy of the satisfaction note, the tremble was missing.

I handed him the dubious signature and asked him if he recognised it.

'It's mine,' he said, unable to see the difference. When I pointed it out, he took a magnifying glass from his pocket to look at it.

'How long have you used that?' I asked him.

'Ever since I lost my glasses,' he said. 'It was some time ago.'

As we finished our meeting, I couldn't help thinking that Mr Sharpe was the victim of a cleverly thought-out scam by a calculating woman. The problem was to prove that Linda Sharpe had been dishonest. I anticipated that she would say she had acted with Mr Sharpe's full agreement, and consequently hadn't done anything criminal. But it was my opinion that any civil court would sympathise with this man, and I resolved to have her brought into the proceedings as a second defendant. The trouble was finding her.

In the meantime I wrote a detailed letter to the loan company, suggesting in no uncertain terms that Mr Sharpe had been duped. I asked for an explanation to persuade me against the view that their representative had been involved, and also what commission had been handed over to the person who had clinched the deal for them.

Fortunately, the hearing was before a Registrar in Chambers. This means that you appear in an office with the Registrar sitting at a table; it is fairly informal and you aren't required to wear robes. We had prepared an affidavit stating our case, and the Registrar adjourned the matter to enable us to apply for legal aid and file a full defence.

Throughout the hearing, Mr Sharpe didn't utter a word, but sat with his head bowed. It would be fair to say that the experience terrified him. He was an old man who had never been in a court before, and the thought of losing his house only increased his torment.

Over the next three weeks we applied successfully for legal aid, sought advice of Counsel, and filed a full defence, alleging misrepresentation and also joining Linda Sharpe into the proceedings. The press got wind of the story, and Mr Sharpe gave them an interview. He was mentioned on a local news programme, and many people who watched it had enormous sympathy for him.

The following day I received a telephone call from an unnamed person who had seen the programme and told me where Linda Sharpe was living, so I was able to have the court papers served. The next day I received an irate phone call from Linda Sharpe herself, who had taken exception to the news item because it had 'blackened her name'.

'I think you're a twat,' she said confidently.

'Many people do, but I can live with it,' I replied, and put the telephone down.

SEVEN

ALBERT STRIKES AGAIN

'The courtroom on line one,' said a harassed Tracy in reception.

'Put them through,' I replied, keen to create the right impression.

'You've got two this morning, Steve,' said the gaoler. 'One's McIver, and the other's called Cusack.'

'What have they done?' I asked.

'McIver – minor theft,' said the gaoler, rustling his papers, 'and Cusack – drugs, possession and supply. A pleasant little mix for your delectation,' he said cheerfully.

'I'll be down by nine-thirty,' I said. 'I want a good clean start today.' I left the office with a spring in my step. I liked being self-employed; it really suited me.

'Morning Oscar,' I shouted at the toilet door.

'Morning, Steve. Kelso's Lad, Doncaster four-thirty, has a fair chance but not much more. I'm having a fiver on it.'

When I arrived at the court, I banged on the large green door to the cell area. A makeshift sign had been placed on it saying 'Tradesman's Entrance', and some wag had scrawled 'Gents' underneath. Weeds had grown around the path, concealing a well-planted rose garden, which was supposed to placate the inmates' visitors while they waited to go in.

The five cells, each ten feet by eight with stone walls, were early Victorian, and in over 150 years of use I don't think they'd changed at all. A wooden bed dominated the floor, and in a corner one of the oldest wcs I've ever seen, covered in graffiti among which was scrawled 'Crippen crapped here'. My first client, Michael Wellington McIver, who was facing three charges of shoplifting, had been put in Cell 1, whose toilet was even older than the office one, and didn't flush at all. Usually, this cell was reserved for awkward prisoners; after two or three hours in there, only the most obstinate or those with no sense of smell continued their recalcitrance. In summer the cells were cold and in winter they were freezing, and only when they were full did the temperature increase: then they became like the Black Hole of Calcutta. It was hard to believe that they were still being used in the 1980s.

He walked into the interview room looking rather downcast, a poorly nourished youth with short mousy hair, spots, and an abundance of gums dominating his large mouth. He was distinguished, however, by the appalling tattoos that covered his entire face. His forehead bore the words 'FORD CORTINA MARK IV', a favourite vehicle for local villains. The largest tattoo was of a spider, sitting in an even larger web which extended from his cheeks to his neck. There were small spiders around his chin, completing a family portrait.

'Sit down, young man,' I said. 'Now, let me get some details from you before we go any further. What's your full name?'

'Michael Wellington McIver, The Children's Home, Wilson Road, Rotherham,' replied the youth.

'And what do your friends call you?' I asked.

'Spider!' he shouted, almost triumphantly.

'And why do they call you that?' I asked, trying to break the ice with a joke.

'Because ah've got spiders tattooed on me face,' said the youth, missing the point entirely.

'Very well,' I said, 'I'll call you Spider too. Let me see your charge sheets.'

He reached into his jeans pocket and pulled out four pink sheets, stained with gravy from the police-issue mince and onion pie served up the night before. I picked them up gingerly: there were three charges and a bail sheet.

'Why are you in custody?' I asked. 'These aren't the most serious offences in the world.'

'I've not paid my fines, so there's a warrant out for me. I'm hoping tha can get me out.'

I realised that Spider wasn't really a bad lad, if misguided, and I actually felt sorry for him – the state of his face, he must have been the butt of every wag in Rotherham.

Just then the gaoler reappeared. 'Have you a minute, Steve?' he asked. 'There's a phone call for you.'

I excused myself, and went out into the main cell area. It was always annoying to get calls when in the cells. You have to break off and run the risk of someone nicking your interview room. There were only two, and if they were occupied you had to use one of the cells, with your notebook and legal aid forms perched precariously in your lap.

'Yes?' I demanded. 'What is it?'

'Steve, is that you Steve?' the caller said. 'Steve Smith, solicitor?'

'Yes I think so,' I said sarcastically. 'But then who else could it be – General Jaruzelski, Anwar Sadat or John DeLorean, perhaps?'

'Steve, is that you?' repeated the caller.

'Oh my God,' I thought. 'WHAT – DO – YOU – WANT?' I shouted slowly and deliberately.

'It's me, Jack,' said one of my best clients. 'It's Albert. 'E's buggered off like, disappeared, legged it… 'E's not locked up, is 'e?' asked Jack. 'Madge is doin' her nut.'

'Not down here, Jack,' I answered, more sympathetic now. 'You keep looking, and meet me here in half an hour if he hasn't turned up by then. I'll get the car out and we'll look for him.'

'Aw reet. I'll paste him when I get 'im,' said Jack illogically.

I went back to the interview room to find Spider picking his nose. He stopped as I entered. 'Will I get bail, Mr Smith?' he asked.

'All being well, Spider,' I said. 'Now sign these legal aid application forms.'

Spider hesitated as I passed him a biro. 'Um… Mr Smith? Tha sees, I can't write reet good. I'm going to learn proper, tha knows, when I get t'chance. Mrs Evans at t'ome promised me.'

I didn't want to embarrass him any more that he already was, so I pointed to the place for him to make a cross.

We left the interview room, and Spider headed back to Cell 1. 'Does he have to sit in there?' I asked Roy, the gaoler. 'Can't he go in one of the others?'

'Sure,' said Roy. 'Come on, me old cock, Suite Two for you; in you go.' Spider went in and the door was closed firmly behind him.

'Next, please,' I said, and a young man in his mid-twenties was brought out. He was wearing the latest designer tracksuit, expensive trainers, the obligatory gold medallion and a gold earring, had blond-streaked hair, and well-manicured fingernails. His arrogance almost shouted as he greeted me, and I took an instant dislike to him.

'Gary Cusack,' he said, and rather pompously handed me his business card. 'Now then, Captain, you've got to get me out of here pronto. I'm sharing a cell with weirdos. Just look at that moron with the tattoos – Christ, what a wacko! Look, get me bail, right, and there's a drink in it for you. You look like a lad who likes a drink.'

'Really? Let me see your charge sheets,' I responded unenthusiastically.

'Ripped them up, old son,' said Cusack. 'The pigs offended me, so they went to Bogville.'

'Who?'

'The filth, the feds... Christ, don't you know any of the names for the cops?'

'No, of course not,' I replied. 'I've only done the job for seventeen years; I must have missed them.'

Cusack was bright enough to recognise sarcasm. 'Hey, you're a cool dude,' he said. 'Come on, let's cut the crap and do the business. I want bail. You do your job, and everything in the garden will be rosy.'

'I need the charge sheets,' I said. 'Wait here and I'll see if the gaoler has copies.'

Roy gave me copies of Cusack's charge sheets from the 'out tray' on his desk, a cardboard box which had housed Lurpak butter in its better days. (The 'in tray' was an empty Andrex toilet-roll box.)

I read them: Possession of cannabis; possession of cannabis with intent to supply; possession of amphetamine sulphate with intent to supply.

'What were the values of the drugs?' I asked.

'Two and five thousand pounds respectively,' said Roy. 'That's weed and speed. Hey, that rhymes,' he realised triumphantly.

I returned to the interview room to find Cusack sitting with his feet on the desk, showing off his expensive trainers. 'Well?' he asked. 'What's the crack? Am I going to get bail or what?'

'Probably or what,' I said. 'Bail isn't likely, as these are serious offences, but I'll do my best.'

Mr Cusack wasn't pleased. 'Your best better be good enough,' he said, losing a little of his 'cool'. I didn't reply, but took as many details as I could and left. At the top of the spiral staircase I bumped into the court sergeant, who was having difficulties with his police radio.

'What's up, Ted?' I asked.

'Don't know, someone's buggering about with the radio. Hello,

hello, court sergeant, courthouse, over. Bugger it,' said Ted, tapping the battery.

Entering the courtroom, I discovered that the Lord Chief Justice was sitting. This was my private name for the magistrate known generally as 'Big Ed', a paranoid schizophrenic who viewed his position as second only to God. He was disliked by court staff and magistrates alike for being the biggest know-all in Rotherham, and was to manners what Attila the Hun was to origami. Ted described him as an 'insulting pillock' and Jack as 'an out-and-out bag of shite'. He ruled the court with a rod of iron, wouldn't allow talking in court, rebuked solicitors if they didn't bow deeply enough, and loathed defendants, no matter what they were charged with. He was the worst bench in Rotherham, and I had got him that morning.

'Bloody marvellous,' I thought. 'I'll need a miracle to get bail today, and I need my miracle quota to help Jack find Albert.'

I walked to the Solicitors' Bench, only to find Philip Portman, the hardest of the Rotherham prosecutors, was prosecuting and big Geoff Clarke, another awkward bugger when that way inclined, was the clerk. What a hand I'd drawn!

When the Bench retired to consider a case, I approached the clerk. 'Good morning, Mr Clarke, and how are you this bright sunny morning?'

'What do you want?' he asked sharply.

'How about putting my case in Court Two?' I asked bluntly.

'Why on earth do you want to go there, Mr Smith? It wouldn't be the choice of Bench, would it? Or perhaps it's the prosecutor you're trying to avoid?' he said sarcastically.

'No,' I said. 'It's the bloody clerk – dark. The light in here gives me migraine.'

'You need a brain to get migraine,' ventured Portman smugly.

'I didn't ask you for your contribution, shithead,' I shouted.

'Now, now, Mr Smith, if you're looking for favours you'll have to watch your tongue,' Portman smiled, and rubbed his hands together, preparing for battle. It was obvious he was looking forward to his morning's work, as he enjoyed helping to lock people up and actually liked the 'Lord Chief Justice'.

'Two prosecutors today, then, Philip?' I ventured. 'What with you and him,' (pointing to the chairman's position on the Bench), 'you won't have to break a sweat, will you?'

'What odious little pieces of waste are you representing today?' he asked. 'You'll never get them out, I'll see to that.'

To say he was biased was an understatement, but Portman was actually a clever prosecutor, and with a Bench like the Lord Chief he was virtually home and dry. He did have a weakness, however, which was that he had a tendency to go OTT, and when he did so, he completely lost his credibility. Therefore, the only chance I had of winning was to make him lose his temper. I already had a knack of doing that, so it was certainly worth a try.

The Bench returned just as Ted's radio started playing up again. 'What's that noise?' shouted the Lord Chief.

'I apologise, Your Worship,' said the sergeant. 'I'm having a problem with my radio.'

'Well, turn it off in court,' said the Lord Chief.

'I'm supposed to leave it on for emergencies,' protested Ted.

'TURN IT OFF!' ordered the Lord Chief.

'Here comes a complaint from the Police Authority,' I thought. But the clerk spoke quietly to the Lord Chief, who at the end of the conversation scowled at Ted over his horn-rimmed spectacles.

'Turn it back on,' I told Ted. 'Round one to you.' Ted did so, scowling back.

'Call my first case,' said the Lord Chief, much to the annoyance of the other members of the Bench, who thought that it was their case too.

'If you please, sir,' said Geoff, 'Michael Wellington McIver.'

Dwarfed by two burly police officers, Spider would have looked insignificant but for the tattoos. The Lord Chief looked at him with disdain and disbelief as the clerk went through the charges one by one, and spider pleaded guilty to each.

'What an obscene object,' said Portman. 'What possible use to society could that be? He ought to be put out of his misery.'

This was my chance. 'Of course the police were less than honourable with the lad,' I offered with a wince. 'You see, they forced a confession out of him. They realised he's an inadequate, and amused themselves by seeing what they could get him to admit to.'

'How dare you?' said Portman, grasping the bait firmly. 'I know that officer; his character's beyond question!'

'By you,' I said provocatively. 'He's a bully.'

Portman rose to his feet and set about a vindictive character assassination of Spider, concluding with a flourish: 'And the true nature of this person's character is to be seen from his denial of the crimes, despite his previously chronicled admissions. I submit to you that bail is inappropriate in such a case.'

I rose to my feet. 'Your Worships,' I announced, 'I am at a loss to understand my friend's suggestion that my client denies the offences. My client has already pleaded guilty. Moreover, these are minor offences of shoplifting, not grand larceny.'

Portman stared the stare that said 'You bastard!' He was right, but the best was yet to come.

Spider was given bail and returned to his cell pending confirmation that the children's home would have him back. Portman threw down his pen, and the Lord Chief saw him do it. 'Mistake number two,' I thought.

Seizing the opportunity for a fag and a tea, the Lord Chief Justice retired, and I went into the Court corridor. Jack was there, his grin gone and concern etched on his face.

'We can't find the little bastard anywhere,' he said pathetically. 'If some bendo's got 'im, I'll kill 'em, I mean it.'

'Don't worry, Jack,' I said reassuringly, 'we'll find him. I've got one more bail application, and then I'm with you.'

Returning to the court, under pressure and contemplating my next bail application, I was approached by a very attractive young woman. I guessed she was about twenty, blonde, with a model figure and pale blue eyes which dominated her magnificent face. Her clothes were expensive and tasteful; a pair of Armani sunglasses adorned the crown of her head, above a platinum blonde fringe which nestled intoxicatingly against a suntanned brow.

'Are you Steve Smith?' she asked.

'Yes, madam. What can I do for you?' I replied.

'I'm Siobhan Danvers, Gary Cusack's girlfriend,' she said with upper-crust self-confidence. 'Are you Steve Smith, his solicitor?'

Why would such a beauty as this, with breeding and style, choose to associate with that shitbag? I wondered, depressed. I admitted that I was Steve Smith.

'Will he get bail?' she asked, nervously twisting a Gucci watch around her left wrist.

'I'll do my best,' I said.

'Thank you, Mr Smith,' she said seductively. 'Can I see him before he goes into court?'

'I'm afraid not,' I replied. 'He's in the cells at the moment. But I'm sure you can see him afterwards if he doesn't get bail.'

'You mean he might not be released?' she asked. I wanted to say 'Not likely,' but she was clearly besotted with the flash git, and I didn't want to upset her more than necessary. 'If it's a question of money,' she protested, 'I have money. I can stand bail, but I can't use my own address.'

Everything fell into place. She was obviously a rich kid living with well-heeled parents too busy to check on their daughter; plenty of money on offer as long as she doesn't bring problems home! I didn't try to disabuse her of her folly, as I doubted she'd listen, and went on into court.

'Are you ready, Mr Smith?' asked the clerk.

'As ever,' I replied, wishing I were somewhere else.

'Gary Cusack, Numbers forty-five to forty-eight, Your Worships,' said the clerk. Portman rubbed his hands together. I could almost hear him thinking, 'Vengeance is mine, sayeth the Lord.'

Cusack was brought in. 'Is your name Gary Cusack?' asked the clerk.

'Yes, sir,' said Cusack respectfully. The clerk read out the charges, and then Portman went to work.

He began a beautifully argued opposition to bail, but unfortunately for him went a little too far. He told the bench what they had to decide – and no magistrate appreciates that, the Lord Chief least of all. Portman had made a big mistake, and I was waiting like a predator who hadn't eaten for days.

Wallop! – A lengthy address appealing to the Lord Chief Justice's obvious good sense resulted in Cusack being bailed, against all the odds.

'The man's a retard,' exclaimed a disappointed Portman, referring to the Lord Chief Justice. I wished I could have saved that victory for a client I liked. Even when you get a result, it isn't always the right one.

Back in the cells, I found Spider and Cusack at the gaoler's table signing for their property. Spider was mesmerised as he watched Cusack slip his Rolex watch over his wrist and have a bundle of £20 notes counted onto the table. 'Two hundred and forty, two hundred and sixty, two hundred and eighty, three hundred,' said the gaoler.

Then Spider moved forward to collect his belongings. 'Twenty, thirty, forty, sixty-eight pence,' Roy said. 'One watch without strap and a brass crucifix.'

'Don't spend it all at once,' said Cusack. 'Here, take this, get yourself a hot dinner!' Cusack handed him a £5 note, enjoying the hero-worship the money and his baubles had brought him. 'Come on, ugly,' he said. 'I'll give you a lift. Where are you going?'

'To the children's home,' said Spider.

Cusack turned to me. 'Nice one, Steve. I like your style. Just send me an appointment and I'll come to see you.'

Spider put his cross on the property receipt form, and Cusack smirked, amused by the admiration of this peculiar youth with the disgusting tattoos.

'Here's your bail sheet, Spider, and don't forget when you have to return to court. If you don't show up you'll be arrested and kept in custody,' I warned him.

'OK, Mr Smith,' said Spider, 'and thanks for getting me out. I won't let you down.'

Within a minute or two they were both released. I returned to the court corridor to find Ted swearing into his radio.

'What's up?' I asked.

'We've found the problem. Some kid's broken into a police car at the compound, and is buggering about with the radio.'

'I thought the compound was secure?'

'It's supposed to be,' shrugged Ted. 'After thirty years in the force, nothing surprises me any more.'

Collecting my papers from the solicitors' room, I looked out of the window to see the beautiful blonde in an open-topped MGB sports car parked outside the entrance to the cells. Two young men got into the car, one in the front and one on the dicky seat: Cusack and Spider. The car took off, and Spider fell backwards onto the seat with his feet in the air. I doubt he had ever been in a sports car before.

As the car disappeared, Ted arrived. 'Steve, you're wanted at the police station. They've caught the kid in the compound, and he's asking for you. He won't even give his name without you present, so I can't tell you who he is.'

'How old is he?' I asked.

'About eight or nine,' said Ted.

'OK, I'm on my way.' Picking up my papers I walked into the court corridor. 'Jack,' I shouted.

'Yes, Steve,' said Jack, who was sitting nearby.

'You'd better come with me. I think we've found Albert.'

EIGHT

I DRESS UP AND THE OAP GETS HIS OWN BACK

We'd been soldiering on with Eric Sharpe's case for some months, with exchanges of court papers and correspondence with the loan company's solicitors. Linda Sharpe had instructed her own solicitor, and my correspondence file had become three inches thick. As the hearing date drew nearer, we had briefed counsel to attend and do the speaking part, as I'm never too confident appearing in the County Court (and also always have difficulty with the detachable wing collars, which I can never fasten properly when I'm in a rush). The hearing had been fixed for the following month, but we weren't sure which day, so couldn't be sure my counsel would be available. I had tried to arrange it as a 'fixture', which means the date is fixed weeks in advance, but it hadn't proved possible.

Sure enough, the night before the hearing the barrister's clerk rang me to say that my counsel wasn't available the following morning. I was left with two choices: to commit suicide, or to deal with the case myself. The first option didn't appeal, for I was only thirty-two and had a wife and a child to support, but the second seemed very little better.

I phoned Eric to tell him the bad news, and he gave me some confidence by saying that he'd rather I did it anyway. Nevertheless, I began to feel that dull ache in the pit of my stomach that tells you all is not well. I read the papers over and over again until at 3am I thought it was time to turn in, but still couldn't sleep for worrying.

It was worse when I arrived at the court building and saw that the television cameras were already there, and since Eric had arrived with a large number of well-wishers, the courtroom would be absolutely packed.

I asked Eric how he was. 'I've got butterflies in my stomach,' he said pathetically.

'I've got giant bats in mine,' I said, even more pathetically.

'Ee, but you cum 'ere every day. You're only kidding me,' said Eric.

'Of course I am, Eric, don't worry; you're in safe hands,' I said, with all my fingers crossed.

There was a knock, and a rather large – and from the state of his robe and colour of his wig, very senior – barrister I'd never met before appeared in the doorway. My eyes nearly popped out of my head when I saw he was carrying about nine law books. He told me he'd travelled from London to deal with the case, and asked to speak to me about it, so we went into a side room.

'You have absolutely no chance at all with this defence, I hope you know that,' said the Rumpolean character patronisingly.

His attitude offended me, and I was in no mood to be bullied. 'If I thought that I wouldn't be here, would I?' I replied.

Rumpole continued, 'If you chuck your hand in now, we won't ask for costs.'

'I'm legally aided,' I said. 'That's the least of my worries.'

'Are you calling any witnesses?' said Rumpole.

'Only the defendant,' I said.

The barrister laughed smugly and went about his business. Eric was relying on me, so I took a deep breath and marched into court. The press occupied a full row, and the public gallery was almost packed. Rumpole came in and sat on the Advocate Bench, opposite me, his well-worn gown bearing all the hallmarks of one owned by a man who knew his business. My pristine gown had all the hallmarks of an owner who had never worn it.

The judge came into court. He was known as a stickler, which didn't make me feel any better. The first case called involved two solicitors. The judge announced that he had read the papers and found a number of faults, listing them in numerical order – I lost count after number 11. I couldn't help but sympathise with the solicitor he addressed, whose gown looked as new as mine. Standards are kept up in court because if advocates do something wrong or fall below the required standard, they're brought to book. I've no real objection to that, but it can be daunting. My colleague was subjected to a grade three bollocking, and at the end of the case hobbled out of court for a blood transfusion. I sat up as the clerk called Sharpe and Sharpe, took a deep breath, and tried to look learned.

Rumpole rose to his feet and gave a brief summary of the case, and the judge peered at him over the top of his horn-rimmed spectacles and asked, 'Is the matter agreed?'

'I'm afraid not, Your Honour,' said Rumpole, staring at me as though it was my fault.

'How long is this case going to last?' said the judge.

'Four hours, Your Honour,' said Rumpole confidently.

'Four hours!' shouted the judge. 'Have you seen the state of this list?' He then looked at me for my input, fumbling in his papers to find my name, saying, 'Mr er, Mr er...'

'Smith, Your Honour,' I replied. 'I act on behalf of Mr Eric Sharpe, and I believe this matter can be dealt with in two hours, Your Honour,' I ventured, slyly seizing my opportunity to score points.

The judge looked furious. 'Well get on with it!' he ordered.

'Rude git,' I whispered under my breath. As the case opened, I amused myself by drafting a message to the judge: 'We've just found a parrot in my back garden, and it keeps shouting, "Now then, you ugly thick bugger!" I thought I'd better phone to see if it was yours.'

I was disturbed from my musings by the judge, who shouted at me as though I were a butler who had misbehaved. 'Has an attempt been made to settle this or not?' he demanded.

I wanted to say, 'Of course it has, you fat pompous git, but the barrister for the other side is a shithead like you.' I thought that advocates should stick up for their rights, and not be bullied by people trying to lord it over the little man.

'Well?' demanded the judge again.

'I regret we're not prepared to settle, Your Honour,' I said, stumbling over my words and forgetting my complaints about humility. 'My client won't back down.'

'Then call the evidence,' said the judge, throwing down his pen.

The evidence was called, and the representative of the loan company came into court. He gave his evidence clearly and concisely, with the air of a man who had given evidence many times before. He explained that he had been approached by Mr Sharpe for a loan, had been to the house and interviewed him, and that Mr Sharpe had signed all the documentation and fully understood the implications thereof. He mentioned that Linda Sharpe was also present, although he was satisfied that the transaction involved only Eric.

The judge said, 'Yes, Mr Smith?' and I stood up to cross-examine.

'Did you have any contact with Linda Sharpe?' I asked.

'No,' came the reply.

'But she was present when you made your visit to the house. Are you telling me she didn't take part in the conversation at all?'

The witness paused before answering, clearly choosing his words carefully, and the judge noted the delay. 'She may have said something, but I don't remember it.'

I then produced the document with the untrembling signature E. Sharpe on it. 'Will you look at this document and tell me what the signature says?'

'Something Sharpe,' he replied.

'No, it's not something, it's an E. Isn't this the note Linda Sharpe signed at the house saying that she understood the loan conditions?'

'I dealt with Eric Sharpe,' said the man.

'What was Mr Sharpe's condition on the day he signed the documents?' I asked.

'He was very well, quite chirpy in fact. He was talking about going on holiday to the coast somewhere,' he said confidently.

'How is it that you can remember such a detail, but you can't remember any conversation with Linda Sharpe?'

'It's just one of those things,' he smirked. 'You remember some things and not others.' I decided to let him continue, because I believed that his offhand manner wasn't impressing the judge.

'Did you know that shortly before this transaction Mr Sharpe had had a stroke which left him dependent on medication?'

'No, but then that's nothing to do with me.'

'No, it isn't. But it's a very strong mediation, which makes him slow to understand what is going on around him. But you didn't find he exhibited any of these problems?'

'No,' said the man. 'He seemed all right.'

'Can you explain to me why you went back the following day?' I asked.

'I don't recall that I did,' said the man.

'Well, let me remind you,' I said. 'You went back because Mr Sharpe hadn't signed the satisfaction note. He was in bed ill and couldn't sign, so you asked Linda Sharpe to sign the form on his behalf, didn't you?'

'No,' replied the man.

'Did you deliver the cheque yourself?'

'Yes,' said the man. 'He was absolutely delighted, like a kid with a new toy.'

'What date was it when you delivered the cheque?'

'The ninth of August,' said the man. 'I have it here in my work log.'

'And you're absolutely certain you gave the cheque to Mr Sharpe in person?'

'Yes,' said the man.

I handed him a letter from the Rotherham District General Hospital, which confirmed that from the 7th to 11th August, Eric had been an in-patient there.

Sweat started to appear on the witness's brow, and he asked for a glass of water. 'Pass me that log,' said the judge. The clerk handed it over and he looked at it. 'You have got that date in this book, and a signature accepting the cheque.'

The judge passed the book to me, and I compared the signature with the untrembling signature on the documents. It was interesting that the receipt for the cheque looked the same as the signature without the tremble. I checked back to the signature following the representative's first visit to Eric's house, which did display the tremble.

I explained this distinction to the judge. He was unhappy at going into areas of styles of handwriting because he thought that was a matter for an expert, but he seized on the differences in Eric's signatures, and asked the witness a number of pointed questions before asking me to continue.

'Eric Sharpe didn't sign the satisfaction note which said he understood what was involved in signing the loan, did he? And please remember that you're on oath.'

Throughout my cross-examination Rumpole had not interfered, and indeed if he had, I think that the judge would have stopped him. But I think he too realised that there was something amiss. When I had finished, he completed his case, and the judge said he wished to hear from Eric. I called him into the witness box and he gave his story, apologising as he went for taking his time over it. The judge was sympathetic, and I took the view that he believed Eric.

Before Rumpole could start his cross-examination, the judge asked, 'Is it true that you knew you were signing for a loan?'

'Yes,' said Eric, 'I knew perfectly well.'

'Did you know when you were signing the documents what the implications were?'

'I didn't know that if Linda didn't pay I'd lose my house. It's all I've got; I can't work any more and I only have my pension. I simply wouldn't risk my home.'

'No,' said the judge, 'I appreciate that. Thank you, I have no further questions.'

Rumpole cross-examined Eric, who at one point became extremely mixed-up with his answers.

'You appear to be rather confused, Mr Sharpe,' said Rumpole.

'It's not surprising,' interjected the judge. 'Your questions have confused me as well. Isn't it the case that Mr Sharpe was confused about the loan too?'

'No,' said Rumpole. 'We don't accept that contention, but of course it is for Your Honour to decide where the truth lies.'

'Quite so,' said the judge. 'Have you any further questions?' giving the clear impression that he had heard enough.

'No, Your Honour,' said Rumpole, and took his seat.

After we had summed up our respective accounts, the judge retired to consider the matter, and Eric and I went to the WRVS canteen. I was still wearing my gown, winged collar and tabs, which delighted the criminal fraternity waiting to go into the magistrates' court in the same building. But before we could drink our tea the usher called us back into the courtroom. Though I was confident of the result, it didn't stop the bats from flying around in my stomach.

The judge summed up the case carefully, and I followed an imaginary swingometer, veering towards us when we had a good point, then away when the other side countered it. But finally he told us he didn't accept that Eric Sharpe knew the implications of what he'd signed, and accordingly found that there had been misrepresentation. His decision would therefore go in favour of the first defendant. I took a deep breath, stood and thanked the judge, and asked for an order for costs.

'Granted,' he said. There were some cheers from the back of the court, and a round of applause. I turned to Eric, who hadn't understood a word of it.

'What's happened?' he asked. 'Have I kept my house or what?'

'I'm delighted to tell you, Mr Sharpe, that not only have you kept your house, you've won your case.'

I went to the advocates' room to change, and when I came out I couldn't see Eric anywhere. The usher told me he'd gone outside, where I found him on a wooden bench near the court with his head in his hands. He was in tears.

'I can't believe it's over,' he said. 'I never want to go into a court again.'

One of his friends came forward and shook hands with him vigorously before leading him off to the car and back home. Eric would sleep well that night, knowing that the threat of being homeless had finally gone away.

It's always a tremendous feeling to win a case, particularly when you believe in it, and I liked to think that in Eric's case I had struck a blow for the little man. It was no great discovery or magnificent effort on my part, just a case of an unscrupulous loan shark in pursuit of his commission at any price – and indeed, if it had been Eric's signature on the satisfaction note, the result might have been very different. But this case underlined my faith in our Legal Aid system, which, although not perfect, was certainly better than anywhere else in the world, and gave Joe Public a more equal chance. Over the next few years that eroded as the system fell into decay and disrepute.

About a month later, I opened the office door to find Eric Sharpe standing there with a heavy shopping bag, completely out of breath. As I ushered him into my room, he was already excitedly gabbling out his story.

We sat him down and he handed me a letter from the loan company, which said, amongst other things, 'In all the circumstances of this case, we do not propose to seek any repayment from you in respect of this loan. We hope that this action will go some way to compensate you for what has happened.'

'Well done, Eric,' I said, and Wilf agreed.

Eric pulled a bottle of champagne from his bag: Wilf fetched two glasses and one broken cup, and we toasted his good fortune (I got the cup).

'Steve,' said Eric, 'I'll never be able to repay you for what you've done, but I'd like you to accept this little gift,' and he handed me a nicely wrapped object. I opened it to find an expensive Waterman pen.

'I love pens, Eric,' I said.

'Yes, I know,' said Eric. 'I've noticed you using a different one every time I see you. Whenever you use that one, you'll remember my case.'

He drank his glass of champagne, then made his apologies, as he had a pressing engagement.

'Anywhere nice?' I asked.

'Yes,' said Eric, 'I'm going out to lunch. The widow next door but one's asked me round.'

'Well, best of luck,' I said as we shook hands again, and Eric turned to leave.

'You want to get an office with a ground floor,' he said. 'Walking up and down these stairs is enough to kill me.'

'That's a good idea, Eric,' I said. 'In fact we're already thinking about it.' Wilf and I had been discussing only the other day how overcrowded we were getting.

The last I heard of Eric, he was happily married to his widow friend. They sold their respective bungalows and bought a ground-floor flat in a sheltered housing complex, with a warden and all the facilities they needed but no loss of independence. His health had improved enormously, so he was able to get about and enjoy life a lot more. Shortly after the house-warming, to which we were invited, I received a postcard from Barbados which read,

'Having a marvellous time – suggest you visit this beautiful island, but avoid limbo dancing like the Black Death – yours Eric and Violet – Thanks again.'

And I still use the Waterman pen to this day.

NINE

I FIND THE LAKE DISTRICT AND SPIDER FINDS DRUGS

Space Invaders was all the rage that summer, and we set up a rented console in the 'boardroom', alias the attic, which was air-conditioned, as the roof still had several holes in it. One lunchtime, we were organising a championship for our friends and associates, and I was opening some beers when Jarvis – who I firmly believe could smell beer at a thousand paces – dropped in to say he'd got a brochure for a hotel in the Lake District, which might suit us for a weekend break with our families.

The Old England Hotel at Bowness on Windermere pro-claimed itself a 4-star hotel with a swimming pool and 'beauty and relaxation facility', still a novelty in those days. Jarvis extolled the virtues of these – which was rather odd, because he didn't swim and I couldn't imagine him going for manicures or massage or any of the other 'treatments' the brochure mentioned. But by the end of the lunch-break, we'd decided to book in for an autumn break, my first holiday since starting the business.

When I got home that evening and told Jennifer, she was initially delighted: after all, given that I hadn't had a break all year, neither had she. Then I told her Jarvis and his partner Anne would be with us, and she wasn't. 'Oh, I see,' she said, 'it's just an excuse for a boozing expedition.'

'Not at all,' I said, rather hurt by her cynicism. 'It's to give us both a break enjoying the rugged scenery of the Lake District in all its magnificence.'

'It's a boozing expedition,' she said, but laughing. 'Never mind, I look forward to it just the same.'

The day soon arrived, and we were due to set off, Jennifer and I and Jarvis and Anne, on the Thursday afternoon. (We did ask Rebecca if she wanted to come, but she intuitively asked who else was going, and when I told her the Jarvises, replied, 'Oh, a boozing expedition.' Since my father had recently bought a new stereo, she unhesitatingly chose to stay with her grandparents instead.)

Unfortunately I didn't finish in court until 1pm, and when I got back to the office there was an urgent brief to counsel to deliver to Sheffield. I phoned Jarvis, and arranged to pick him up on my way home, so he could help load the car while I showered and changed. We would then call at Sheffield with the brief on the way to the Lakes.

The barristers' chambers in Sheffield was an 'olde-worlde' building, with several brass plates by the door, and the brief was for Peter M. Baker, one of the best, and therefore busiest, barristers around. We met in reception, and he introduced me to his new pupil, a recently qualified barrister by the name of Alan R. Goldsack. Little did I know then that I was to spend the next twenty-five years or so working with him, learning a great deal in the process.

On the road again, we'd only got as far as Leeds when Jarvis said, 'I'm going to have to pay a call.' I thought that he wanted to use the toilet, but he wanted a drink. Jarvis on holiday avoids sun, beaches and sightseeing, preferring to spend his time in an air-conditioned bar. To keep him happy, we picked a local pub and had a bar meal before we continued our journey. After a two-and-a-half hour drive, we arrived at Windermere around 5pm. It was a magnificent sight, with the sun glittering on the water. I asked Jarvis to admire the incredible view, but there was no answer, and looking in the mirror, I saw he was fast asleep. Anne and Jennifer just looked at each other and shrugged.

Fifteen minutes later we were at the Old England Hotel, and having parked the car and unloaded our belongings, made our way to the front desk. It was a traditional hotel, and I liked it immediately. We were shown to our rooms, which were on the same floor, and having unpacked met the Jarvises in the bar.

The bar led to a veranda overlooking the lake, with a magical view of the boats bobbing about on the water. There and then, I vowed that one day I would have my own boat on that lake. We spent the early evening browsing around Bowness, and inevitably ended up at one of the boatyards, where I was totally captivated by the cabin cruisers. Making our way back to the hotel, we saw one of the boats that ply the lake mooring up, and all agreed on a boat trip – particularly when Jarvis saw a sign proclaiming that the boat was licensed.

As I looked to the shore on our way to Ambleside, I saw cottages dotted around the lake's edge, slightly above the level of the water. I had been in the Lakes for a little more than two hours, and had already decided that one day I would buy a boat and cottage here. All I had to do was to convince Wilford, a building society and a bank – and, of course, Jennifer.

Back at the hotel, we arranged to meet at 8.30pm for dinner. Jarvis said he'd have a nap, and the women went off to the 'beauty and treatment centre', where Jarvis had paid for the treatment of their choice. Beforehand they both opined, forcefully, that this was an excuse to get them out of the way while we boozed, but when they returned, Jennifer having had a massage and Anne a manicure, they were delighted, and full of praise for Michael's generosity. I used the time sitting on the veranda watching the boats, then went down to the dining room to book our table. The window tables were all booked, the head waiter said, but a £5 note and telling him Michael was the first son of a baronet miraculously got us one. We ended the evening with the wine waiter bidding 'Sir Michael' goodnight.

Jarvis, confused, said, 'He called me Sir Michael. Is he taking the Mickey?'

'Probably,' I said, and helped Anne get him back to their room.

The following morning, Jarvis was dragged to a lake-view seat for breakfast by an ingratiating waiter who constantly called him 'Sir Michael'. I noticed we were the only guests who had our luggage carried out to the car when we left!

On Monday I was back in the office bright and early, to face a long list of prisoners demanding bail. Spider was locked up again, and this time the offence was more serious – he had been caught in possession of amphetamine sulphate, commonly known as 'speed', and the drug squad didn't believe it was for his own use. The case was adjourned for what's called a three-day local, to facilitate interviews – an excellent device in the prosecution's armoury to gather evidence and seek confessions, and Spider wasn't equipped to deal with it. In court he looked nervously around the public gallery to see who was watching, which I found worrying, because it wasn't usual for him. Then I saw his gaze fix in one position with real fear in his eyes. He was looking at a man with dyed blond hair and a diamond in his ear, wearing an expensive designer suit. Cusack.

During the adjournment, I went to the cells to see Spider. 'What's going on?' I asked. 'Why were you carrying all those drugs? That's not your game.'

It was almost as if Spider had been programmed. He addressed me in a slow, monotonous tone. 'They're mine, for my own personal use.'

'You don't use drugs, and if you did, you had enough there to supply the whole of your estate. What's going on, Spider?' I asked again.

'They're mine,' he repeated. 'I'm taking the rap.'

'You know the police are saying you can only have that quantity if you're going to supply it? They're going to charge you with possession with intent to supply, which is very serious. I don't believe they're yours; I think you're carrying them for someone.'

'I can't grass,' said Spider.

'I'm not saying you should grass on anybody, Spider, but the court won't believe they were for your own use, and I think they'll convict you of possession with intent to supply. With that amount of drugs, it means the Crown Court and a big sentence.'

'What do you call a big sentence?' asked Spider.

'Well, even though there are no drugs offences on your record, I think you're going to be sent away for two years.'

Spider gulped, clearly shocked, but refused to change his story. I left it at that, and agreed to come to the police station when the drug squad were ready to interview him.

I went back into court and finished my last case. When I came out into the corridor, Cusack and his pretty girlfriend were waiting to speak to me.

'I see poor old Spider's in bother, then,' said Cusack.

'What's that to do with you, Mr Cusack?' I asked.

'Just interested,' he said. 'He works for me now.'

'Doing what?' I asked.

'Well I'm selling cars, and he valets the motors. He's good at it. Admittedly he can't do any more than that, because he only has half a brain. He fetches parts for me and generally runs about.'

'Well' I said, 'you're right, he's in bother,' and turned to walk away, but Cusack and his girlfriend followed.

'Well,' I demanded, turning to face him, 'what now?'

Cusack tried to put me on the back foot by saying, 'You don't like me, Mr Smith, do you?'

'I'm not paid to like people, Mr Cusack,' I replied. 'I do a job, to the best of my ability, whether for you, Spider or anybody else.'

'OK, Captain,' said Cusack. 'By the way, has he said anything about me?'

I'd wondered when we would get to that, but wasn't prepared to enter into discussions with filth like Cusack. 'Spider hasn't been interviewed at length yet, but that's going to happen over the next two or three days,' I said.

'Oh, I just wondered,' said Cusack. 'Somebody's got to have a bit of time for the dickhead. Listen, call me if you need anybody to stand bail for him.' This time he produced a metallic card with the words 'Cusack's Cars' and in brackets after it 'Value for money, every car guaranteed.'

'I'll bear it in mind,' I said, and turned away.

As I moved downstairs, I saw Cusack getting into a flashy sports car. He drove off at speed, screeching his tyres. 'Flash git,' I thought, and went about my business.

Back at the office, my clients had arrived for their 2pm appointment. Calling them in, I was greeted by two men and a woman, all middle-aged and, by the look of them, related. All three were well dressed and respectable-looking. The woman, who introduced herself as Mrs Cartwright, was extremely businesslike and presented a leather folder with a file of documents inside. She told me that they wished to obtain a Power of Attorney over their absent brother's estate, so that it would be administered while he was unavoidably absent.

'There shouldn't be any difficulty about that,' I said. 'But I will need to see your brother to make sure he understands the implications and get his signature. In what way is he incapacitated?'

Mrs Cartwright explained concisely that the four of them were partners in a thriving business, of which the elder brother, Brian, was the senior partner/managing director. But the previous year he had begun to exhibit behavioural problems and bouts of depression, and was eventually committed to a mental institution for his own welfare. It wasn't possible to carry on the business properly unless the partners could make day-to-day decisions on

Brian's behalf, so their bank and various creditors had suggested that they obtain a Power of Attorney. Apparently Brian was in full agreement with this course of action, and the doctors had agreed that he understood it.

I just had one niggle of doubt: I didn't know these people, who were from out of town, so I asked why they'd sought me out. They said I'd been recommended by another client of mine, and they had ventured out of their normal area because of the embarrassment this family difficulty had caused in the local business community. It seemed a satisfactory explanation, so I agreed to prepare the documentation, then visit their brother and report to them on the meeting.

At this point the police rang, saying they were ready to interview Spider. With a full appointments list, I took my next client with me to discuss his case on the walk to the police station, leaving Wilford to deal with another. The criminal law doesn't work to solicitors' convenience. One day you can have a very light diary, and the next you're hit with everything at once.

I was met by the detective inspector of the drug squad, wearing a bomber jacket, jeans and training shoes. They dress like this to blend in, but he still looked to me like a police officer in a bomber jacket, jeans and trainers. I was surprised to be greeted by someone of that rank, until the inspector explained that he was investigating what he believed to be a large drug ring operating in Rotherham.

'We're not sure about the extent of McIver's involvement. However, he was seen to collect a large parcel in Sheffield and travel over the Rotherham boundary. The surveillance officers following him became concerned they'd been spotted, so we had to stop the car and arrest McIver before he got any further. We really wanted to follow him to his final destination, but were worried that he might try to dispose of the drugs in some way.'

'I simply can't accept that Spider is a drug dealer,' I said.

'We're not saying he is,' said the inspector, 'but he's involved, and we want to know to what extent. He's either an errand lad or the real thing. The problem is he won't tell us, and in the absence of any explanation we have to conclude that he's a dealer.'

'In the absence of anything else, why couldn't he just be a user or an errand lad?' I asked.

The officer smirked. 'Well, it's for him to convince us he's not the main man.' It seemed obvious to me that the inspector knew Spider was an errand lad, and hoped he was going to help him catch bigger fish.

I was allowed a few minutes with Spider before the interview, and immediately waded into the attack. 'What in God's name are you playing at, Spider?'

'I ain't done nothing, Mr Smith,' said Spider. 'Only what I was told.'

'Well, now the police are going to interview you, Spider, and you don't have to answer any questions if you don't want to. But if you do answer, the police will be entitled to use what you've said in evidence later. Exactly what is your case?' I asked.

'I've got nothing to say,' he said.

I asked him if he was afraid of anyone, and he said he didn't want to say, but he obviously was. There seemed little point in continuing our conversation, because Spider wouldn't open up at all.

The inspector came in with an aggressive-looking detective sergeant, who spoke with a sneer. He had the job of note-taking, and the inspector asked the questions. (At that time the police didn't use tape recorders for interviews; usually the questions were put and the subject's replies written down contemporaneously. It was a laborious process, and the police thought it unfair, because it gave the defendant time to think about his answers.)

'Where did you get the drugs from?' asked the inspector, staring into Spider's eyes. Spider was uncomfortable and looked away. It was standard police procedure to stare their subject out, to unnerve the interviewee and thus get the answers. 'If you don't explain to us what you know, we'll take the view that you're the main man,' said the inspector.

I objected to the line of questioning, and told him I wished my objection to be registered. The sergeant took umbrage, and threatened to have me excluded from the interview if I interrupted again. I said that in that case, I would advise Spider not to answer any more questions.

The inspector frowned him down, and began to question Spider more sympathetically. He did his very best to catch him out, and I was surprised at the way Spider responded, as if he'd been coached. He denied that he was going to sell any of the drugs, and the inspector put it to him that such a huge quantity of drugs couldn't possibly be for his own use. Spider refused to answer, and I winced in the certain knowledge that he was going to be charged with possession with intent to supply.

The interview took two hours, and I had been listening so intently that I'd forgotten about the appointments waiting for me back at the office. Anne had done her best to reschedule them, but some clients weren't happy and had waited to complain, so I spent some time apologising to a waiting room full of disgruntled people. One of them was an old lady from a local old people's home, complaining that the man in the room next to hers had Alzheimer's disease, which somehow prompted him to expose himself on a regular basis, and my aged client was sick and tired of it. I could hardly consider taking court proceedings over this, so I rang the matron in the hope that she might be able to sort something out. She was very sympathetic, and agreed to move the ageing Romeo to another floor. One satisfied customer!

The following morning I was back in the office, making arrangements to see the gentleman in the psychiatric hospital, when the police phoned to say they were placing Spider before the court that day. I was able to dash over to see him in the cells before his case was called. He looked dreadful, pale and drawn but highly excited, twitching and behaving in a bizarre manner. I realised that he had become addicted to amphetamines, and was obviously in a state of withdrawal.

In the court corridor I noticed Cusack, in intense conversation with a man who looked like a heavyweight wrestler. I dodged past him and went into the court. I asked the prosecutor what application he intended to put forward, and told him I would be agreeable to any conditions of bail. Unfortunately, he said that he couldn't agree bail; Spider had been re-interviewed in my absence, at his own request, and admitted that he had purchased the drugs and was going to sell them himself.

I was horrified. 'But the police told me they didn't believe he was a supplier!'

'Yes, I understood that to be the case, but Spider apparently was most insistent that they were his drugs, and because there was no evidence to the contrary, he's been charged with mainstream supply.'

I went back to the cells to see Spider, and he couldn't look me in the face.

'I'm sorry, Mr Smith, but it was me, so I've admitted it.'

'Who were you going to supply?' I asked him.

'Anybody. Round the pubs and youth clubs, like,' said Spider, with so little enthusiasm that he was clearly lying.

I looked at him, and asked, 'What have you done?'

Spider looked back at me, and simply said, 'I've saved my neck.'

I knew he was taking the blame for somebody else, who had threatened him with consequences that frightened him more than prison. I was annoyed that this could happen – and, more importantly, that there was nothing I could do about it.

When I came upstairs, I saw the sergeant, and said, 'You know those drugs aren't his, don't you?'

'Mr Smith,' he replied smugly, 'your client says they are, and we can't prove any different, so there it is. If we ever find any evidence to the contrary, we'll act on it, and then he can be prosecuted for perverting the course of justice.'

I didn't argue, but simply said, 'A brilliant bit of detective work, Sergeant, you should be very pleased with yourself,' and walked off.

I went into court a most unhappy man, and in no position to argue with the facts as the prosecutor read them out. I did apply for bail, however, although I didn't believe that Spider had much chance. I pointed out that he had no previous convictions for any drug matters, and all the drugs in his possession had been recovered, went into some detail about his background, and even ventured my opinion that he was no more than an errand lad, despite his admissions. The court were unimpressed, and promptly remanded Spider in custody. I noticed Cusack nod to him as he was led away to the cells.

I went back to the office to find a phone message from the children's home, enquiring about Spider's welfare and very distressed about the allegations. The matron told me that Spider was highly regarded at the home and, despite that stupid tattoo business, he wasn't a bad lad. She believed that he had been used, saying that he was easily led and often fell prey to unscrupulous people, and offered to come to court the next week to guarantee Spider a home.

TEN

AM I HEADING THE RIGHT WAY FOR THE PSYCHIATRIC HOSPITAL?

I had never been to this psychiatric hospital before, and despite plotting the route and being a seasoned traveller, I lost my way. Coming across two locals drinking beer outside a pub, I asked them for directions.

The one who did all the talking looked to be in his early 70s, with shoulder-length, iron-grey hair and matching shaggy eyebrows which joined in the middle. His jet-black moustache had clearly been dyed, and he wore a tweed sports jacket with green cavalry twill trousers and well-worn brogue shoes.

'Am I heading the right way for the psychiatric hospital?' I asked.

'It depends, do you hate your mother?' asked the man seriously.

'I want to get to the psychiatric hospital, can you point me in the right direction?'

While he explained the route, his friend just looked up into the skies as if waiting for some visitation. He was younger, short-haired and clean-shaven, smartly dressed with highly polished black shoes and a pair of horn-rimmed spectacles only partly concealing steel-blue eyes. I always believed that I was a good judge of character, and I assessed that this man had the air of a doctor about him.

About half a mile down the road I spotted a dark, austere

building set amid trees, and thought that might be what I was looking for. I turned up the drive, only to find that it was a private house. The owner was none too pleased to be asked if his home was a psychiatric hospital, but he set me in the right direction, and at last I came across a splendid-looking building in extensive grounds, with a long winding drive leading up to it. It was a magnificent place, with immaculately tended rose-beds set in a sea of emerald grass.

At the reception area I gave my name and showed my identification to a pleasant lady in a smart suit. She said I was expected, but asked me to fill in a form confirming my identity and the reason for my visit.

The reception area was beautifully decorated, full of flowers artistically arranged in crystal vases, which caught the sun shining through the window. The receptionist confirmed that all the flowers were from the hospital's own gardens, and proudly explained that some of the 'non-risk' patients worked in the gardens, and kept them beautifully neat and tidy. There can be no doubt that first impressions count, and the gardens and reception area made a very good one on me.

On the walls hung a number of excellent sketches and paintings. 'Are these done by the residents as well?' I asked.

'Oh yes, all the paintings you see in the hospital are by the patients.'

My attention was drawn to a neatly printed sign which offered tea and coffee for people who were waiting. 'Do you have catering staff for the refreshments?' I asked.

'Oh no, all the refreshments are prepared by the patients. Would you like something?' she queried.

'No thank you,' I replied, remembering that the last murder case I had dealt with involved poison, and the defendant had ended up in a psychiatric ward.

About five minutes later a young lady in a nurse's uniform came to fetch me. I followed her through the double doors from reception into the hospital itself, and the atmosphere changed completely. We went through a series of security doors, all of which had to be locked behind us, to a hexagonal reception area, all wooden panels and plate-glass windows, which housed a series of television monitors with the names of the wards underneath. One man was watching the monitors, another was watching him, and a third watched me as I was booked in.

'Sign here,' demanded a gruff and unfriendly voice.

'Only if you promise to let me out again,' I said, trying to bring some levity to the proceedings, but the man just looked at me. 'I wonder if the patients man reception as well,' I thought, as I followed on through the security doors.

Eventually, I arrived at Trueman Ward, where I was eyed suspiciously by two orderlies in white hospital jackets. I explained whom I had come to see and why, and was asked to wait in a small interview room at the head of the ward. As I sat down I saw a closed-circuit camera focusing its attention on me. I realised my friend from the booking-in point would be watching me, and couldn't help but smile. 'Watch it, Smithy,' I thought, 'you'll be kept here if you're not careful.'

As I waited, a man who looked like a patient walked past the door, peered in, and advised me not to take the medication as it had 'gone off'. Someone shouted 'Bernard!' and he left. Then a gentleman who appeared to be in authority approached me. He courteously told me that my client would be brought to see me within five minutes, and offered me tea and a scone, which I politely declined. 'They must work the patients to death,' I thought. 'Either that or they're all cooks.'

However, he was as good as his word, and my client arrived within a few minutes. Introducing myself, I shook his hand and invited him to take a seat.

Brian was over six feet tall and in his early 50s, with sandy hair streaked with grey, discoloured pale blue eyes, giving me the impression that he could be an alcoholic, a deep resonant voice, and the bearing of an ex-serviceman. He seemed relaxed, and told me that he had been expecting me because his brothers and sister had called earlier in the week. He thanked me for coming, and with some embarrassment explained that it was in the interests of the business for him to sign the Power of Attorney. He seemed perfectly rational to me, so I asked him about his health.

Brian said he was making good progress because of the medication he'd been given and the lack of pressure from being away from his job. He thought the prognosis was good, and it might not be too long before he could leave here and get back to work. I suggested that this might put him back in the same position as before, but he told me he planned to take on extra help to ease the workload. He spoke a good deal of sense, and I couldn't help thinking that if he was crackers, then I was a Dutchman.

I took the documents out of my briefcase and explained them to him in detail. He had one or two questions, and when he was satisfied with my answers asked to borrow a pen to sign the documents. Looking out at the beautiful gardens as I reached in my pocket for my Parker, a leaving present from my colleagues at the old firm, I asked if he had been involved in any of the work, but Brian said the gardens were out of bounds for him, which didn't worry him because he suffered from hay fever.

When Brian saw it was a fountain pen he at first demurred at using it, on the grounds that it was unwise to let anyone else write with one's fountain pen because the pressure and angle would be different, which could ruin the nib. I told him I didn't think one signature would matter, and handed him the pen.

I gaped with astonishment as he scraped it viciously down the paper, spattering ink everywhere. He then calmly handed the document back and asked, 'Have you seen my blotting paper?'

At this point a male nurse, who had been watching from outside, came into the room and took the pen from Brian, who looked perplexed.

'What's wrong?' he asked. 'I was talking to Mr Smith; we were having a very interesting conversation.'

'Nothing, Brian, but I think you should come with me now,' said the caring nurse. 'It's time for your medication.'

'Oh, all right,' said Brian. He stood up, offering his hand, and said, 'Well, thank you very much for coming, Mr Smith, I'm most grateful for your kind assistance. I do hope we'll have the opportunity to meet again, and perhaps you'd like to undertake more legal work for me in the future. Bye for now.'

Still open-mouthed, I shook hands on automatic pilot. He left the room, and I looked down at the pen nib, which was split beyond repair, glanced at the document with the scrawl and puncture marks on it, and got up to leave.

I was escorted back through the same doors and along the corridors to the booking-in area. 'Going out?' said a gruff but familiar voice.

'Yes,' I replied, the wounded pen still in my hand. 'Yes, I'm going now.'

'You're not stopping, then?' said Gruffy.

'Not today, maybe next time,' I said, entering into the spirit of the occasion, but thinking, 'Not on your life.'

As I waited at the gate, a patient accompanied by a male nurse passed me. 'Who are you?' he asked. Still in shock, I turned slowly to face him and said, 'My name is Van Damm, I'm from Holland.'

He replied, 'Lovely place, Holland. I used to do a lot of mountaineering there.'

'Of course you did,' I said, and was released to the public areas.

Outside, I noticed the old character from the pub picking himself a rose for the lapel of his jacket. 'Found your way, then, old chap?' he said.

'Yes thank you,' I said, and tried to walk past him as quickly as possible, my earlier experiences of strange people rattling around in my head.

'Have you been to see an inmate?' he asked chattily.

'Yes,' I said, and walked on, but he had clearly decided to accompany me to the car park. I must admit that I was a little concerned at having inherited another nutty hanger-on, and was thinking of ways to shrug him off, when a nurse hurried towards us shouting, 'Doctor, doctor! Come quickly; we have an emergency!'

I looked around to see whom she was speaking to – and, to my surprise, it was the old man she was addressing.

'Very good, Nurse, straight away. Cheerio, old chap,' he said to me.

'Cheerio,' I said, and whispered under my breath, 'My name is Mr Van Damm, and I'm a mountaineer from Holland.'

I must have said it louder than I thought, because a nurse walking past paused and said, politely but firmly, 'Are you a resident, sir?'

'No, but I think I may be one day,' I replied, smiling. I hurried to my car and drove off. As I looked in my mirror, I could have sworn I saw her writing down the registration number. Or was it just paranoia?

ELEVEN

I MISS THE CHRISTMAS PARTY BECAUSE JIMMY SHOT HIS WIFE

Christmas is a special time of the year, and in 1981, our first as self-employed men, Wilf and I decided we would have a superb time. We organised another Space Invaders championship, and planned to invite guests to the office for a drink on Christmas Eve, to show our appreciation of their support during the year.

'Who do you think we ought to invite?' mused Wilf.

'How about Pagey?' I said.

'Not likely,' said Wilf. 'We'll get barred.'

'Oh, he's not that bad,' I said, 'and if we politely ask him to behave…'

'He'll do exactly the opposite,' Wilford interrupted.

'We've got to invite Jarvis,' I said. 'Let's draw up a guest list.'

As we walked across the landing to our office, I heard the sound of the trombone. 'Morning Oscar,' I shouted.

'Morning, Steve,' came the voice from within, then a further blast.

'Morning Oscar,' said Wilf.

'Morning,' said Oscar. 'Three-thirty Haydock Park, the Windygulch Kid.'

'How appropriate,' I said. We checked our pockets to find that we had almost £5 between us, and decided to put this princely sum on Oscar's horse.

'We've got to invite Bodge,' said Wilf. 'And anyway, I want him to look at the roof.'

'Fine, so long as you don't let him touch it,' I said. 'What about the Mad Scotsman?'

As we were making our plans, the barrister's clerk in Sheffield rang. 'You have the attempted murder case of Riley, Mr Smith,' he said. 'We're thinking of putting it in on the twenty-third of December.'

'But that's bound to run on to the next day, which is our office party,' I protested. 'We've got all our friends coming.'

'Oh,' said the listing officer in a wounded tone, 'you're asking me to leave this man in prison over Christmas so you can have your office party, is that it?'

'I don't know why you're moaning, Tom, you're invited,' I replied.

'Oh, in that case,' he said, 'we'll start it in January.'

We both laughed, but of course our party had to take second place to an attempted murder trial. One positive aspect of the case was that I would be working with a barrister I'd admired for many years – Wilfred Steer QC, from Newcastle, a highly regarded counsel in his mid 50s. I had briefed him for Jimmy Riley's case some time before, and his clerk had promised that the case wouldn't be listed unless he was available. The junior counsel was the Alan Goldsack I'd met on our way to the Lake District, who was beginning to carve out a niche for himself in the local court scene.

Jimmy Riley was on remand at Armley Prison in Leeds, charged with attempting to murder his wife and his best pal Patrick Guthrie, who had apparently been having an affair. Although Jimmy had been told this was going on, he had chosen not to believe it, since Patrick was his best pal and he trusted him.

However, on the night in question Jimmy had decided to go home unannounced to satisfy himself that the rumours weren't true. Unfortunately he took along a loaded twelve-bore shotgun, something not considered unreasonable in that part of Rotherham.

The prosecution case was that Jimmy had gone to the house with intent to shoot – an intent reinforced when he looked through the lounge window and saw his wife, naked, locked in a passionate embrace with Guthrie, who was wearing only a black T-shirt. Our defence was fairly simple: Jimmy contended that he only meant to push the gun through the window to frighten them, but it had gone off accidentally. He did accept that his actions were reckless, and that he was responsible for the complainants' injuries, so we suggested that he should plead guilty to a lesser charge of wounding. The prosecution had refused to accept this plea, so there had to be a jury trial. If Jimmy were convicted of attempted murder, he could go to prison for ten years, whereas for the lesser charge, taking into account all his mitigation, five would be nearer the mark.

It seemed fairly obvious to me that if Jimmy had a finger on the trigger when he pushed the gun through the window, the impact could well have set it off, depending on how sensitive the trigger was. We enlisted a firearms expert, a retired Army officer, who made a number of tests on the weapon, simulating the incident. He demonstrated that the weapon had a hairline trigger, meaning that the slightest pressure on it would result in the gun going off.

I phoned Wilfred Steer QC with the news. He was delighted, but cautiously pointed out that if the defendant only meant to frighten the complainants, why put his finger on the trigger at all? I set off for Armley at the earliest opportunity to put the question to Jimmy.

Jimmy's reply was simple. 'There was nowhere else to put it, and that's the normal way I hold a gun. I was just thinking about them, not what part of the gun to touch. I never gave a thought to the trigger. I also knew the safety catch didn't work, but it certainly wasn't on my mind that night.'

I'd got my answer, and now it was up to Wilf Steer.

By now there were six of us in the office, as we'd taken on another typist. Kimberley had a lovely smile and even nicer personality, which kept the local yobs quiet in the waiting room, but she wasn't very good at spelling, and never thought about the sense of what she was putting on paper. In her first week she committed three classic howlers, two of which I'd asked her to sign on my behalf and send out, so didn't spot in time to avoid embarrassment.

The first went to the Lichfield Magistrates' Court, in mitigation for a Rotherham haulage and scrap firm for an overloading offence. I dictated, 'I act on behalf of AB Limited, a small haulage and scrap firm in Rotherham.' The typed version read, 'I act on behalf of AB Limited, a small haulage and crap firm from Rotherham.' Quite what the magistrates thought of that, I've no idea.

The next was a real winner. I'd written to the director of Public Prosecutions, querying whether a murderer was fit to plead, and ended: 'Clearly the public interest will determine which course will be adopted, etc, etc.' Kimberley typed 'Cleary the public interest will determine which course will be adopted, excreta, excreta.' When I read the copy, all I could say was 'Oh, shit.'

The third error was of my own making. I had to write to an obnoxious bloke at the Legal Aid Board, a man who would argue black was white just for the hell of it, and acted as though he personally was the custodian of the country's legal aid monies. He'd challenged a reasonable bill, and I'd dictated a letter stating my annoyance. I finished it: 'So I object to the taxation, which I believe is unfair and unreasonable,' and added an aside I thought might amuse my permanent secretary, Sheila, who knew the character in question, 'You great fat arsehole.' But I'd forgotten the letter would be typed by Kimberley, and so it read, 'And so I object to the taxation, which I believe is unfair and unreasonable, you great fat arsehole.' Luckily, by this time I'd learnt to check her typing before it left the office, or I might never have got a legal aid claim passed again!

The day of Jimmy's case came. Mr Steer appeared, wearing an old and well-worn coat, carrying a worn-out bag holding a tatty wig and gown. He was tall and distinguished-looking, with a deep, resonant voice, an RAF-type moustache, and sharp eyes that eagerly took in all around him. There was a notable contrast between the clothing of Mr Steer and our junior counsel Alan Goldsack, the older man with huge experience and all the tricks of the trade, and the young one with the new gown and white wig.

When all our team had assembled, we went down to the cells to see Jimmy – who, as one might expect, was extremely nervous, since there was an awful lot at stake. Mr Steer went through Jimmy's evidence thoroughly before we went back up to take our places in Court Number 1, which was a traditional courtroom, with a dock decorated with brass rails. The judge entered, the jury were sworn in, and the clerk of the court put the charges to Jimmy, who pleaded not guilty in a loud, clear voice. The prosecutor opened his case and then called the evidence.

We could have agreed his wife's evidence, but knew she'd be a bad witness and not impress the jury, and we were right. We did have certain points to put to her, not least that the gun went off at the moment it went through the window. I doubt if she knew the relevance of that question, but she agreed with the proposition, making our explanation more likely.

Jimmy's best pal hadn't turned up, so the prosecution tried to adjourn the case, but were ordered to proceed because the court had information that he had left the country to work abroad, and hadn't left a forwarding address.

The pendulum began to swing our way, and at the end of the prosecution case we were doing well. We then had to decide whether or not to call Jimmy. He'd given an account of the incident to the police, and we didn't disagree with what he'd said, so there wasn't much more he could add, apart from why he'd had his finger on the trigger. But Mr Steer felt that he could deal with that in his final speech to the jury, so he wasn't called. We did call the gun expert, however, who did an extremely good job.

The best of the case was saved for last: Mr Steer's speech to the jury, which ended with his suggestion that, whilst Jimmy was guilty of wounding by reason of recklessness, it was certainly not attempted murder. As he sat down, I could almost hear the people in the gallery applauding, such was its impact. The timing was first-class, because we had reached 1 o'clock, so the jury would adjourn for an hour's break with his words ringing in their ears.

The afternoon was taken up with the judge's summing-up, which had a heavy prosecution bias. But I've found that if a judge sums up heavily on one side, whether prosecution or defence, juries sometimes tend to go the opposite way. They went to consider their verdict, but by 6 o'clock hadn't reached a decision. The court adjourned, and the next morning at 10am I visited my client in the cells. He was in reasonably good spirits, and grateful for the work we'd done on his behalf. At noon, the jury was still out. I went down to see Jimmy again, and he took a deep breath when he saw me because he thought a decision had been made. I put his mind at rest about that, and used the time to do some dictation and make several phone calls to the office, only to be told that the Christmas party was in full swing and Sean Page was delighting the audience with a selection of tunes from Gilbert and Sullivan's *The Mikado*, outrageously out of tune.

'It's a shame you're missing it,' slurred Wilford.

'I think that's an unfortunate and totally inept comment to

make, Wilford,' I said, or words to that effect, and went back to pacing up and down the court corridor. About 3 o'clock I visited Jimmy once again, and found him playing cards with two of the prison officers. He clearly wasn't concentrating on the game, and I felt sorry for him. He wasn't really a criminal, and I hoped he would get off.

Eventually we were called back into court, and the tension mounted as the jury took their places one by one. The clerk to the court asked the foreman of the jury to stand, and a snipe-nosed gentleman in a business suit got to his feet.

'Members of the jury, have you reached a verdict upon which you are all agreed?' asked the clerk.

'No,' said the foreman.

My heart sank. The clerk of the court then asked, 'Members of the jury, have you reached a verdict upon at least ten of you are agreed?' (Juries are entitled to bring a majority decision of not less than ten to two.)

'Yes,' said the foreman.

The clerk of the court added to the tension by shuffling his papers, then asked, 'Members of the jury, on the count of attempted murder, do you find the defendant guilty or not guilty?'

We all listened with bated breath as the foreman of the jury announced, 'Not guilty of attempted murder, but guilty of wounding.'

Jimmy fell back into his seat, and there were gasps from the back of the court, where his family were sitting. Mr Steer's expression didn't change for a second as he continued to write a note on his brief. The judge asked him to address him in mitigation, which he did very eloquently, and then the judge proceeded to sentence.

He prolonged the agony by telling Jimmy that wounding was still a very serious matter, in which he could only consider passing a custodial sentence. He said that he had mitigated it by reason of the circumstances, but the shortest sentence he could pass was one of five years. The judge's final words were 'Take him down.'

With remission for good behaviour, a five-year sentence then was worth about three and a half, and Jimmy had been in custody on remand for about eight months, so he had less than three years left to serve. As he was taken down he gave me the thumbs-up sign, as delighted as any man could be who had just been sentenced to five years' imprisonment. Had he been convicted of attempted murder he would have been sent away for a very long time, so it wasn't surprising that he was grateful.

When I left the court it was after 5pm. The Sheffield Christmas shopping traffic would be at its worst, and flakes of snow were beginning to fall. The office party was due to finish at 5.30, and I saw little point in rushing, because I wasn't going to make it in time.

I walked past a Salvation Army band playing 'God Rest Ye Merry Gentlemen' just as the prison bus pulled out, and I spotted Jimmy waving from the back seat. Corny as it may sound, it was a poignant moment.

I got back to Rotherham just before 6pm to find the office in darkness. Christmas trimmings and plastic string adorned the staircase, and when I put my hand on the banister I touched something soft and horrible – green crazy foam. With a grudging laugh I walked into the reception area, which looked like Hiroshima just after the bomb. The walls were covered with trimmings and there was a Christmas tree in the corner, its fairy lights flashing on and off. In our office I found a number of Christmas cards on my chair. I don't think I'd ever felt as lonely.

I opened a few cards, including one that showed Santa Claus on a roof – but he wasn't delivering presents; he appeared to be removing lead. Inside, it read 'All the very best from Jack, Madge and the kids,' and at the bottom Albert had scribbled his signature with a swastika next to it. There was a card from Mrs Yardley and

Louise, and a very large one, unsigned and with the price label still on it, with the legend 'Happy Birthday, Granny' and a Marks and Spencer voucher for a Pyrex dish inside.

I shook my head, put them all on my desk and decided to call it a day. I got all my things together, picked up my keys, and moved to leave. At the top of the stairs I surveyed our office. So this is my first Christmas party – the bastards could have at least let me know where they going, I thought… And on that thought, the door to Oscar's room burst open and the whole gang jumped out, blowing party trumpets and throwing streamers and shouting 'Surprise, surprise!'

Pagey came to the fore, wearing a Flowerpot Man's hat and an extremely lifelike pair of rubber breasts. 'Merry Christmas, and congratulations on your first Christmas in practice, Steve,' he said, and handed me a small box.

Inside was a wooden plaque with a silver-plated mount which read, 'Wilford Smith & Co., inaugurated 13 May 1981'. I would have been deeply touched, were it not for the fact that I'd bought it the previous week for the reception area. But I suppose it was the thought that counted.

The cassette player started blaring out the hit record of the day, 'The Land Of Make Believe', and Pagey began dancing by the front window, which looked onto the street. He appeared to be simulating the national dance of Nigeria in a rather offensive gyrating fashion. Two policemen on patrol outside looked at the window and simply shook their heads.

'Merry Christmas,' shouted Pagey, giving his front end a squeeze. 'God bless us, every one!'

TWELVE

MONEY ISN'T EVERYTHING – IS IT?

Late February 1982 was freezing cold. The air-conditioned roof was the next thing on the agenda, so Wilford and I were having a partners' meeting to review our finances when Tracy buzzed to say that Sam Trueman was in reception, wanting a quick word with me.

I had known Sam for ten years, as we had played in the same football team until he retired at forty, because his knees had started to go. I remember his retirement party very well because I couldn't remember anything about it the next day, if you see what I mean, but I'm told that I gave a speech and made a presentation. He was a thoroughly likeable chap who spent most of his life either at work or on the football field. At the end of his playing career, he kept in touch by managing one local side and helping train the factory team for whom he had played. He spent the rest of his time working in his garden and studying DIY at the technical college. Sam was immensely popular, and being a bachelor he often shared evening meals with his friends' families, but I was surprised he had called at the office, because he had always believed social visits shouldn't interfere with working hours.

When I invited him in he looked troubled, and I saw that this wasn't a social call.

'What's to do, Sam?' I asked cheerfully.

'I don't know where to start, Steve, but I've got a bit of a problem, and I wondered if you could help me.'

After offering him a glass of Canadian Club whisky, our favourite tipple at the time, I turned up the gas fire and pulled two chairs in front of it. Sam was holding some papers and a large envelope with an unfamiliar stamp, which caught my eye. 'Where's the stamp from, Sam?' I asked.

'Australia,' he replied. 'This is what I've come to see you about. How much time have you got?'

'As much as you need,' I replied.

'I'll need to explain some of the background before this makes any sense. You see, Steve, I'm adopted,' he said, clearly uncomfortable about divulging such personal details. 'I never knew my real parents, only that my mother was well-to-do and from a good family; my father was the eldest son of their gardener. In those days, that wouldn't do at all. He was turned off, she was sent away to have the baby secretly. I only found out much later there were two of us, twins, and we were put up for adoption and split up.

'When my real grandparents died, they left everything to my mother's sister, who emigrated to Australia just before the war and invested it in a farm out there. My adoptive parents told me that when I was about ten, but not about my twin. I suppose they didn't know either.

'Then, about a year ago, a Mr Shoreham called me. He said he'd married a relative of mine many years ago, who had now died, but had made him promise to seek me out one day.

'I must say, Steve, I was thrown, but also intrigued, so I agreed to meet him for a meal at a hotel here in Rotherham a few weeks later. Well, on the day I went to the hotel reception, and almost straight away a man came up to me. "You're Sam, aren't you?" he said without a hint of doubt. I didn't know what to say. He could see I was confused, and led me to the bar, where we had a drink. He said he didn't think there was an easier way of telling me than to get straight to it. "That'll do for me," I said. "I prefer straight talking." But you could have knocked me over with a feather when he said I was his brother-in-law.'

'The twin?' I asked, just about following this.

'That's right,' said Sam. 'He must've seen the shock register in my eyes, because he said, "You didn't know you were a twin, did you?" I told him I didn't even know who my mother was, and certainly not that I was a twin. "Ah well, they didn't know," said Shoreham. "You and Janet were parted at birth, and she was taken straight away, whereas you were left until some weeks later. It was thought best at the time to do it that way. After all, we're talking about forty years ago."'

Sam paused to compose himself, then resumed his story.

'So I had a sister, you see, born ten minutes before me. Like me, she'd never enquired about her birth, until she found she had cancer and hadn't long to live. By that time she'd married Shoreham, but they had no children, so she decided to trace her mother. It became quite a quest, and by a number of twists of fate, they found that she'd married and ended up in America, but unfortunately had died five years before my sister's quest started.

'Quite by chance, they found that our only surviving relative was our aunt in Australia, who was something of an eccentric and didn't want to have contact with them. But their correspondence with her did reveal my existence. As you can imagine, it was very difficult for them to track me down. Unfortunately, Janet passed away just a few months before her husband managed it. It was sort of his tribute to her, to carry out her wishes.'

Sam, clearly moved by Shoreham's efforts, told me that he'd kept in touch with him ever since, and had been to stay with him one weekend. This had been an incredible experience, discovering his family history, about which he'd known nothing for over forty years.

'I'd always wondered, you know,' he said, 'if there might be somebody out there I belonged to. I just wish she'd lived long enough for us to meet.'

'But what's the problem now, Sam?' I asked.

'Well, yesterday I had a letter from some lawyers in Australia, saying they'd managed to track me down following my Aunt Kitty's death – my mother's sister. They say they need to establish that I actually am her nephew, and then I suppose they'll tell me what they want. I hope I'm not going to be asked for money.'

Sam produced the letter, which simply enquired into his identity and requested a copy of his birth certificate, and asked if I'd check it out for him. I agreed to do so. I guessed that the old lady had died intestate, in which case her estate would pass to the next blood relative or relatives. There was no likelihood of Sam being asked for money, and indeed a small windfall might be coming his way.

'It's a fantastic story, Sam. I hope there's a happy ending,' I said.

'Well, Steve,' replied Sam, 'there could have been if I'd been able to meet her, but since the old lady obviously didn't want to know me, will you answer the letters and see what they want?'

We shook hands, and he picked up his belongings and made to leave, then turned and said, almost apologetically, 'There's one thing, Steve. If there's a picture of my mother, I'd like to see it. I've already got some from Janet's husband, but it would be interesting just to see…' His words trailed off as he left the room.

Touched and determined to help him, I wrote to the lawyers that very day. About a fortnight later, I received a reply from the Sydney-based firm, informing me they were satisfied that Sam was Kitty's last remaining blood relative and, since she had died intestate, her sole beneficiary. They were in the process of calculating the value of the estate, and would send further information as soon as possible. They would also phone me on Friday and explain the background more fully.

Friday arrived, and I was given the full story by a pleasant chap called Newbury. Kitty had emigrated to Australia, having fallen out with her family, but inherited their money, which she put to good use by buying a sheep farm. As more land became available she bought it, acquiring a vast estate. But living in the outback, she formed a great friendship with the Aborigines, and over the years gave them a considerable amount of her land. Mr Newbury told me that she had disposed of three-quarters of the acreage to pay off debts and to ensure that the Aborigines, who farmed the site and looked after the sheep, had a permanent home and some security. It would be for Sam to decide whether he kept the farm or sold it. I couldn't see the logic in keeping it, and from the other side of the world said I'd advise him to sell. Mr Newbury then told me that there was another asset that might be more appealing. For the past forty years, Kitty had owned a villa in northern Majorca, a prestigious area – one of the neighbours was none other than Sir Harry Secombe. The villa was set in three acres, had two swimming pools and a Bentley in the garage, plus a bungalow occupied by the maid/housekeeper and her husband, the handyman, who had been employed for almost thirty-five of those forty years. It was fully furnished and valued at some £700,000.

The only other asset appeared to be a collection of a hundred and fifty didgeridoos, of questionable value.

Shocked, and not quite able to believe the fortune Sam had inherited, I thanked Mr Newbury for his clear explanation, and said I'd write with Sam's instructions as soon as possible. I put the phone down, sat back in my chair and thought about the magnificent country of Australia, with its warmth and space, and then about Majorca, with its discreet coves set in an elegant coastline, the mere thought of which made me drool. I realised that I had the welcome duty of informing Sam of his good fortune, and phoned him. There was no answer, so I left a message for him to contact me as soon as he could.

That night, as I was leaving the office, Sam came round the corner in his car. He told me that he had got my message and had called on the off-chance that I would still be at work.

'Park and meet me back here,' I said, unlocking the office door again.

When he arrived I took him into the office and poured him a large whisky.

'Sam, you're going to need this,' I said. 'Prepare yourself for a shock.'

'I'm not paying out a penny piece,' said Sam.

'You're dead right there, old cocker,' I replied. 'Just listen to what I have to say.'

I related the phone conversation with Mr Newbury, and showed Sam the correspondence I'd received. He listened intently.

'You mean there's a farm, and how many acres?'

'Ten thousand,' I replied. 'Most of the land's been sold off or given away to the Aborigines who live there. Apparently the farm's a bit ramshackle, but the land's quite valuable.'

Sam sat back in his seat and asked me to guess how much it would be worth.

'At least a hundred pounds an acre, I believe, but there are some duties to pay, which will probably reduce the value.'

'Bloody hell, Steve,' said Sam. 'It's too fantastic to think about.'

'Well, that's not all,' I said smugly. 'There's also a villa in Majorca with three acres and a swimming pool.'

'Bloody hell,' said Sam, running out of superlatives.

'Actually it has two swimming pools, and a housekeeper's bungalow in the grounds, but I saved the best until last. There's a Bentley in the garage.'

Sam looked at the ceiling, scratched his head, then looked at me rather suspiciously. 'This isn't one of your little jokes, is it? Because if it is…'

'Look, Sam,' I said, 'this isn't something to joke about. You have to face facts, and the fact is that you, Samuel Trueman, are a millionaire. Oh, and you own about fifty thousand sheep.'

'You're serious, aren't you, Steve?' said Sam. 'It's like a dream.' He scratched his head again and said, 'If you weren't so ugly I'd kiss you.'

'Oh, kiss me anyway, you rich bastard,' I said.

We laughed, and I poured him another glass of whisky. We discussed the merits of owning a sheep farm, but Sam was determined to sell it. To ensure that the residents would still have a home, he decided to gift them the farmhouse and some land, which was typical of Sam, and no less than I expected. The only difficult decision was the house in Majorca. We decided that Sam would consider the matter, and make a decision at a later date.

When he did, it was that he would go to Majorca to see if he liked the villa, and he asked me to go with him in an advisory capacity. Naturally I agreed, and after juggling my court commitments, we fixed a date for a fortnight later.

The day before the flight, I luckily had only two cases on my list, which meant I'd be able to get away early. One involved Redfern Keown, a small-time thief much under the influence of his frightening wife 'Our Jessica', a large, overbearing woman who seemed allergic to water. She had greasy black hair, fingernails to match, and a nicotine-stained upper lip: when she spoke, cigarette ash fell down the front of her frock and formed a trail to her waist. Although she wore bottle glasses, according to Redfern she could 'feight', and her tongue could curdle milk.

I was trying to lighten the tone of the interview. 'Our Jessica' was worried about the loss of DSS benefits if Redfern were sent to prison, Redfern was worried about his kids, and I was worried about Jessica, who could well erupt in court if he were given a custodial sentence, and get herself arrested for contempt. The kids would then go into care, and they didn't deserve that. In a nutshell, we were all stressed.

So, reading the report from the Probation Service, I changed the words to try and raise a laugh. 'Unfortunately,' I said, 'the probation officer believes Redfern isn't really responsible for these offences. He commits them to keep his wife in fags and booze.'

I thought this was funny, but Jessica thought the comments were actually in the report, because I'd said it with a straight face. To my horror, she shouted, 'You effing little runt!' and hit him in the face with her right fist, making his nose bleed. Redfern cried, and I felt terrible – as did 'Our Jessica' when she realised it was a joke.

Later, in the first-aid room, Redfern asked me what he should do about his stormy relationship. I advised him to divorce her as soon as possible, but instead he went to prison for two months, and Jessica lost some of her benefits. He came to see me afterwards and I suggested divorce proceedings. This didn't appeal to him, so I suggested that if murder was out of the question he ought to try a trial separation. He didn't like that idea either, so I asked him to reconsider murder – but this time I told him it was a joke.

The next day, Sam and I crossed the tarmac at Palma airport. Transport had been organised to take us to the north of the island, and within two hours we were there. The wrought-iron gates looked newly painted, and a terracotta tile driveway twisted invitingly into the distance. A woman's voice answered the intercom mounted on the gatepost, and the electrically operated gates opened. We paid the taxi and walked up the drive. It went on for ever, with shrubs and flowering trees, many of which I hadn't seen before, on either side: it was a blaze of colour and perfume.

Round the final bend was probably the most beautiful building

I'd ever seen. The terracotta-coloured house was enormous, with two separate patios at different levels, both housing magnificent swimming pools. At the first patio, we could see beyond the trees to the coastline, and a pale blue sea that shimmered in the sunlight. We both stood and looked at the breathtaking view without speaking.

Our silent deliberations were interrupted by a female voice shouting 'Hello, hello.' A grey-haired lady in her sixties, her dark skin lined by the sun, wearing a black dress and oven gloves, approached us with a welcoming smile on her still beautiful face. She shook hands with us both, and curtsied. 'My name is Isi,' she said with a giggle and asked us to follow her.

We were taken to the second patio, which had a number of stone urns containing freshly watered bright red and yellow flowers. My attention then focused on a man who looked like a farmer, wearing a red T-shirt, shorts and sandals. He was about the same age as the woman, and clearly the handyman. When we were introduced, Toni raised his hat and we shook hands.

Isi gave us a conducted tour of the house with great enthusiasm. She spoke fairly good English, which was fortunate because we had no Spanish at all other than *paella, muchos gracias*, and *habla Inglés?* It was beautifully decorated and extremely well maintained, and she was clearly justifiably proud of it. Toni took over to show us the grounds, which included their cottage with its own vegetable, herb and fruit gardens.

Afterwards, we sat on the patio and looked out to sea, eating the meal Isi had prepared, washed down with a litre of local wine. It was an idyllic spot, and I could understand how Kitty would have been intoxicated with it.

We had all but forgotten the Bentley when Toni showed us a three-door garage, and there it was in all its splendour. It must have been twenty-five years old, but in mint condition with only twenty thousand miles on the clock. It was a white open-topped car, but hadn't been used for a considerable time, so would need a mechanic's eye over it before we were able to drive it.

Isi explained that the local village, some two kilometres away, had two restaurants, a mini-market, an electrical shop and a newsagent's/post office.

'What more do you want?' said Sam enthusiastically, and I realised that he was smitten.

The next two days were spent enjoying the house and the locale. We helped Toni in the garden, and spent the early evenings in the pool, although Sam suffered some skin reaction to the substance in the water, the equivalent to our chlorine. The evenings were spent dining in grand style on the patio. The marvellous cellar included a lot of expensive champagne, it was still warm enough to sit out in shorts and T-shirts, and we took full advantage of both facts. I was sorry when it was time to leave, as although we had only been there two days, it was easy to get used to the life.

On the flight back home, Sam told me that he wanted to put his own house up for sale, and as soon as he had dealt with his affairs, catch a plane for Majorca and make the Villa 'El Anos Poca' his new home. I couldn't blame him. Three weeks later I was waving him off at East Midlands airport with a standing invitation to visit. As he boarded the plane, I realised that I'd never seen him so happy. Driving back to Rotherham, it was raining and cold and I couldn't help feeling a touch of envy.

When I got back to the office, I was told that Spider's case would be heard the next morning before the Crown Court. Reality was certainly waiting for me with open arms, and I embraced it reluctantly.

THIRTEEN

CIGAR ANYONE?

The next morning, the usual smoky haze in the court corridor seemed thicker than ever. Then the smell hit me, and I realised that most of the people sitting along the corridor were smoking large cigars.

Before I could get into the solicitors' room, I was stopped by four clients all speaking at once.

'Who's first?' I asked. The biggest of the group, a lad called Fingers, was 6'6" tall and weighed about nineteen stone. It was no surprise to me that he indicated that he was first, and had a new charge of GBH (grievous bodily harm). The giant announced that he was definitely not guilty because, to use his own words, 'I only hit him once.'

'Yes,' said his friend, 'but it was with an iron bar.'

'It depends on the nature of his injuries,' I told him. 'If they're serious, then obviously that would reflect in the charge.'

'Wha's tha' mean, reflect in the charge?'

'Well, if he has serious injuries, then taking these into account together with the fact that you used a weapon, that's probably why you've been charged with such a serious offence.'

'He deserved a crack,' said the giant. 'he's an eapa.'

I hadn't heard this term before, and I asked, 'What's an eapa?'

'Tha knows: eapa shit.' The giant spelt it out slowly. ''E'S A 'EAP OF SHIT – AN EAPA, GET IT?'

'Oh, I see,' I said. 'Give me your charge sheet.' As I looked at it, he lit a cigar, which looked suspiciously like a Havana.

'Does tha want wun?'

'No thanks,' I said, 'I don't smoke.' I completed his legal aid application, which he signed with a cross, and he went and sat in the smoke-filled corridor.

I followed him out to call my next client. 'Tom Gifford,' I shouted at the top of my voice.

'Argh,' came the reply. I went back into the room and sat there waiting for him to appear. After about half a minute I got up and called his name again. 'Tom Gifford,' I shouted.

'Argh,' the voice said.

'Where are you?' I shouted.

''E bain't 'ere.'

'Well why did you answer his name?' I asked.

''E's me mate,' came the reply. Confused by that, I tried someone else.

'James Beresford,' I shouted. This time I was going to wait to see if he appeared. He didn't. 'James Beresford,' I repeated, 'Are you there?'

'No,' came the reply. 'But 'e's me mate as well.' I entered into the spirit of things and shouted, 'Well, is anybody here?' to which the entire corridor shouted 'Yes!'

I then noticed a familiar figure walking towards me through the smoky haze. It was Jack, and with him was Albert the 'Orrible. Jack, too, was smoking a large cigar.

He asked if he could have a word, so I took him into the interview room, leaving Albert to wait outside. 'I didn't know you were in court today,' I said.

'No,' said Jack, 'I've not seen thee about this one yet.' He handed me his charge sheet, which I put into my notebook until I had time to consider it. 'I'm not guilty, and I'm not having this wun. Fair's fair, if I've done owt I'll take it, but not this eapa.' Maybe they were giving the vocabulary away with the cigars.

'I'll complete your legal aid application, then go into court and see the evidence against you, okay?' I said, just as the usher from Number 1 Court came in to tell me that my case there had been called and they were waiting for me. Now I was in for a Grade 4 bollocking. This really dropped me in the 'eapa', for I was needed in two places at once.

When that bench retired, I dashed over to Court 2 and started that case, but within ten minutes the magistrates in Number 1 Court had reconvened and were demanding my attendance. As the usher came in to give me the bad news, I noticed that he had a cigar behind his ear.

'Bloody hell,' I thought, and continued with my case. Fortunately the bench had to retire to consider it, so I ran back into the other court and apologised for keeping them waiting. The chairman, who had a council meeting in an hour, wasn't pleased. I felt like saying, 'For God's sake, man, how can you expect me to work in two places at once?' but he wasn't interested in my welfare, only his meeting.

As he began to deal with that case, the usher from Court Number 2 came in and said that bench were demanding my immediate attendance. I ran across to receive my second Grade 4 bollocking in five minutes, and as I did so, a woman grabbed my arm and thrust a pair of underpants at me, saying, 'Give these to Fred'. Fred was one of my clients in custody, and his wife was using me as the postman to take him clean clothes. I dashed into court carrying a pair of underpants in my left hand. The magistrates looked at me with some disdain, and I stuffed them into my pocket, tendering my apologies.

The magistrate took off his glasses and said, 'You appear to be in a bit of difficulty, Mr Smith.'

'Yes, it's the job, sir,' I replied. 'I appear to be required in two places at once.'

When the case was finished, I dashed back to Court 1 to take the result and present a mitigation. As I was addressing the bench, the lady who had presented me with the underpants put another pair in front of me. I stopped talking and looked at the magistrates, who looked at me. 'Mek sure Fred gets 'em,' she said into the silence. I told her I would, and looked to the bench again. 'And another thing,' I said. 'He's from a broken home, but he's got plenty of underwear.' They laughed, but refused bail and that was the end of that.

Outside, the corridor was even thicker with cigar smoke. I found Jack in the tearoom, deep in conversation with someone I didn't recognise, and called him over. He approached me with his beaming grin. 'Cuppa tea, Steve?'

'Yes please, Jack.'

'Cigar, Steve?'

'No thanks, Jack,' I said. 'But what's with these cigars? Everyone seems to be smoking them.'

'Get away,' said Jack.

At this point the emphysemic usher called me out again. 'There's a man in the cells wanting to see you, Mr Smith. I've got his charge sheet here.'

He passed me the document. I read the charge, 'That you Jonathan Hawkins on the 7th July did steal one African parrot to the value of £900.'

I put Jack on hold again, and went to the cells. When I got downstairs, the jailer asked me if I wanted to see the 'Bird Man of Rotherham'. Before I could answer, he asked 'D'you think he'll get bird?' I gave him a withering look, but he answered his own question: 'Shouldn't think so, it's only a poultry offence.'

Jonathan Hawkins was a swarthy youth with buck teeth and a cleft palate, which left him unable to pronounce certain letters. J became Y, T and R became W, B became M, S became Th, and H wasn't in his vocabulary. He was wearing tracksuit bottoms and a yellow T-shirt with a picture of a bird on it.

'What's your full name, young man?' I said to him.

'Yonathan Aw'ins.'

I realised that we were going to have difficulties. 'And your address?' I asked.

'Wenty woo, Witherthonm Thwee' 'oom, Wothewum.'

'I missed that, give me it again.'

'Wenty woo, Witherthonm Thwee' 'oom, Wothewum,' he repeated.

'Ah yes, Rotherham,' I exclaimed, recognising a word. 'But whereabouts in Rotherham? Could you just write it down for me on this legal aid application?' I thought that was the best way of dealing with the problem, because the lad was clearly embarrassed by his speech defect.

'I'll tell you what,' I suggested, 'I'll ask a question, and you answer yes or no.'

'Eth!' came the reply.

'Did you pinch the parrot?' I asked.

'Eth – er, no,' came the reply.

The hard one first, I thought. 'Have you still got the parrot?'

'No,' he said.

'Where is it now?'

'On,' he replied.

'On what?' I asked.

'On,' he repeated, making fluttering motions with his hands. 'Own away,' he said sadly.

'Oh – gone, flown away?' I queried.

'Eth,' he said.

'Where were you when it flew away?'

'Us!'

'Would that be bus? You were on the bus with the parrot when it flew away?'

'Eth.'

'Why did you take it, Jonathan?'

'Ike awwo's.'

'You like parrots, is that it? Do you know you shouldn't have taken it?'

'Thuppothe.'

'What are you going to plead, Jonathan?' I asked.

'Ilty,' came the reply.

'Yes, I think that'll be best.'

I was exhausted after that interview, and glad to get back upstairs. I couldn't help wondering how on earth he would cope with giving evidence. The prosecution file included a short interview, recorded contemporaneously by the police, and consisting of just four pages – but when I looked at the times at the bottom of the page, it had taken seven hours!

Back in the cigar-laden corridor, I collected Jack and we went into the rat hole, where I searched through my notebook for his charge sheet. 'Let's see what we've got this time, then, Jack,' I said, and read aloud, 'That you, on the 4th July, did steal four thousand Cuban Havana cigars, the property of Ashley Warehouse Limited.'

It wasn't until I got to the end that I actually realised what I'd said. I stopped and read it again, this time spelling it out slowly and deliberately.

'THAT YOU, ON THE 4TH JULY, DID STEAL FOUR THOUSAND CUBAN HAVANA CIGARS, THE PROPERTY OF ASHLEY WAREHOUSE LIMITED.'

Jack looked at me, unperturbed, as he drew on his Cuban Havana cigar.

'Is there any connection between this charge and the fact that everybody in the court corridor is smoking cigars?' I asked.

Jack considered as he blew out smoke, creating the impression of a managing director about to decide on a major share deal. Looking at the ceiling and then at the floor, he drew again, slowly blew the smoke from his mouth, and flicked the ash onto the desk in front of us. 'Tha wha?' he asked.

'To put it in English, Jack, who's been flogging the cigars on the court corridor?'

'Buggered if I know,' said Jack. He added profoundly, 'I think 'e's wrong, tha knows.'

'Who's wrong? What are you talking about, Jack?' I asked.

'Alf,' said Jack. 'Tha knows Alf. That bloke I was talking to in t'tearoom.'

I remembered Jack huddled in a corner, deep in conversation with a man I didn't recognise. 'Oh yes. What's he wrong about?' I asked, thinking that this was the answer to the cigar query.

'Churchman's Joy,' he announced confidently. 'It's got no chance at 'aydock Park, it's too 'eavy.'

I knew from long experience that Jack lived on an entirely different planet, but I was getting extremely frustrated by this time.

'Forgive me, Jack, I wasn't talking about Haydock Park or Churchman's Joy or Alf. I was asking you about the cigars.'

'Oh, them,' said Jack. 'I found 'em.'

'Found them. Where did you find them, Jack?' I asked.

'On the lorry,' said Jack. 'Argh, they were delivering, weren't they, and these boxes were on t'back o' t'lorry, so I like found 'em and walked off. It were like an accident, tha knows.'

'You stole them from the back of the lorry,' I said. 'Is that right?'

'Fair comment, that, cocker, if tha puts it that way.'

Clearly Jack had to plead guilty to 'finding' the cigars on the back of the lorry, particularly since I learned from the prosecution file that he'd been seen 'finding' them by two witnesses from the shop, before they found their way into the sidecar of Jack's motorbike. I began to consider whether I could find any mitigation to put before the court. It would have been helpful if the property had been recovered, but unfortunately Jack appeared to have sold most of them to an eager public.

'They're a good smoke,' said Jack, as if he had done nothing wrong.

The usher then came in and asked me to go into court, since the Bird Man was due to appear.

I wanted to warn the court clerk of the defendant's difficulties, but he wouldn't listen: he had a long list, and was determined to finish by 1pm and have his full one-and-a-quarter hour lunch break. (With luck, I might even find a second or two to have something to eat myself.) 'What's the next case?' he growled.

'Jonathan Hawkins,' I replied. 'Charged with parrot pinching.'

'How long will it last?'

'For ever.'

'I beg your pardon?' said the clerk. I didn't have to reply, because the Birdman had arrived.

The clerk rustled his papers, looked at his watch, and asked, 'Are you Jonathan Hawkins?'

'Eth,' answered the Birdman.

'Well, say so properly,' replied the clerk sharply. 'What's your address?'

'Wenty woo, Witherthonm Thwee', Hoom, Wothewum.'

Here we go, I thought, so I interrupted with the full address. 'Thank you,' said the clerk, looking confused.

The charge was read out, and the clerk asked Jonathan for his plea. He couldn't answer immediately, because of a mixture of nerves and his impediment.

'Well?' shouted the clerk. 'Are you deaf?'

'No, sir,' I interrupted. 'He has a speech impediment.'

'Well why didn't you tell me?' said the clerk, embarrassed, and all of a sudden Jonathan shouted, 'Ilty!'

The prosecutor opened his case, and laughter came from the public gallery when they heard the details.

After I had addressed the court, the chairman of the magistrates asked Jonathan, 'Have you anything to say?' Oh my God, I thought, but before Jonathan could speak, the clerk was in like a flash: it was 12.56pm. It is rare to suffer a long retirement so close to lunchtime, and indeed at 12.59 the bench returned and fined Hawkins £150 and costs.

Most of the lunch break was taken up with Jonathan's paperwork and sorting out how he could pay his fine. I only had time for a cup of tea and a quick telephone call to Wilford back at the office. At 2.15pm, the emphysemic usher went into the corridor to call Jack in, and came back into court coughing from the cigar smoke outside.

Jack had agreed to plead guilty because the evidence was overwhelming, but sometimes it doesn't work like that. Defendants can sometimes simply change their minds, almost as if it's an affront to ask them to plead guilty. This was such a case. When the charge was put to Jack, he said firmly, 'Not guilty.'

The clerk asked me if they were my instructions, and I told him with a sigh that they certainly weren't. 'I thought you were pleading guilty,' I whispered to Jack, as pleasantly as possible through gritted teeth.

'Aw reet,' said Jack. 'I thought I was pleading not guilty.'

'No,' I said. 'You're pleading guilty because you did it and have admitted it.'

'Okay,' said Jack, and I asked the clerk to put the charge again.

'Are you guilty or not guilty?' said the clerk.

'Not guilty,' said Jack then, as I was about to get up again, shouted 'Guilty!' almost as if he'd made the biggest concession of his life.

The magistrates were sharp enough to see that earlier that year Jack had been sent to prison for driving while disqualified, and obviously thought a probation report might give them a better idea of how to deal with the case. The chairman renewed his bail, and Jack left court shaking his head.

'Your client seems a bit confused, Mr Smith,' said the court clerk.

'Not half as much as I am, sir,' I replied, bowing to the bench, and the chairman of the magistrates winked at me, as if to say 'Yes, your job's an eapa, isn't it?'

Outside, Jack was waiting for me with his wife Madge, who was puffing on a large cigar. Albert was standing beside them, a wide grin festooned on his face.

''Ello, Mr Smith, will 'e get nick?' Madge asked.

'I hope so, Madge, I really do,' I said, and they both laughed and left.

'All right, Steve?' said Albert. 'Have a nice day, me old cock.'

I tried to smile, resisting the temptation to clout him at the back of the head. As he turned to walk away, I noticed the remnants of a large cigar in his hand, held behind his back. I shook my head in despair and went into the solicitors' room.

Later that afternoon I put the radio on to hear the latest Test score, and just managed to catch the racing results before the cricket started. The 2.30 at Haydock Park had been won by a rank outsider called Churchman's Joy at 30–1. That night, Wilf and I went out for a Chinese meal on our winnings, making many toasts to Jack and his mysterious friend Alf.

FOURTEEN

WHO WANTS A WILL ANYWAY, AND THE RETURN OF SAM

During that meal Wilf and I decided that, after a good first year, it was time to buy new cars. The next day, we traded in our old cars as deposits on two brand new Ford Capris, with the registration numbers OHE 164X and OHE 165X. There's something special about the thrill of collecting a new car, the smell of the interior and the sparkle of the paintwork, which you remember for ever.

A few days later, we were sorting out our applications for the AA when David Langley, a client of ours, rang to speak to Wilf about buying an old people's home. He and his wife already owned one, which was doing very well, and they'd decided to open a second in a different area. David was an electrician-cum-handyman-cum-dogsbody, and his wife a qualified nurse: their residents couldn't look after themselves and had no relatives to help. Some were sound in mind but physically deficient, and others were physically able but mentally frail.

During the conversation, David said that a number of the residents had expressed the desire to make wills, and asked if we could help. It would be essential for us to visit the home itself, because many of the patients could not travel to our office. We agreed, and set a time for the visit.

By this stage my friend Roy Bennett, a retired police inspector, was helping in the office, taking statements and preparing cases for court, relying on his thirty years' experience as a police officer, and ten as a managing clerk in a solicitors' office. Roy had retired from his last post due to a heart attack, but when he recovered he needed a part-time job to keep him sane. He worked with us three days a week, soon becoming a great asset. Extremely fit for seventy, he looked particularly distinguished, with his white hair and moustache, and would often regale us with stories of his army service in Burma, particularly tales of the Japanese prisoner-of-war camps.

On the day of the appointment at the old people's home, I collected Wilf and Roy from the office, and off we went to take instructions from twelve residents. By dividing the clients between the three of us, we thought a couple of hours would see the job done. We were wrong.

We arrived as lunch was finishing, and David and his staff were busy pouring tea and serving biscuits and scones. David explained to everyone who we were and the reason for our visit, and said that we would speak privately to each resident. We were given a small round of applause, and all three of us nodded and smiled back.

David left us, and I asked who was first. No one answered. I decided they were probably a little shy, so went up to the gentleman nearest to me, who was sitting in a large leather armchair.

'Do you know who I am?' I said politely.

'No,' said the man, 'but Matron will tell you if you ask her.'

'Right. I'll see you later, if I may, sir,' I said, turning to the next in the firing line.

Wilf and Roy moved among the various groups, introducing themselves. Roy was persuaded to sit in a large chintz armchair and remove his jacket. As he sat there chatting, an auxiliary nurse came into the room. She sat next to him and asked, 'You had your bath this morning?'

'Yes,' said Roy, not seeing the relevance of the question.

'Have you been to the lavatory?' she continued.

'Well, yes, but it's not something I want to talk about.'

'Don't be shy, I might be giving you a bed bath tomorrow.'

'Oh, wait a minute,' said Roy, 'I think you have the wrong person. I'm not a resident.'

'That's what they all say,' said the nurse, tugging at his arm.

'But he'll verify who I am,' said Roy, pointing to me.

'Is this gentleman with you?' asked the nurse.

'Never seen him before in my life,' I said firmly, seeing the possibility of a joke. Wilf turned away to hide his laughter as Roy was escorted to goodness knows where.

My next client was in a wheelchair and looked very old indeed, with a heavily lined face but a twinkle in his eye. 'Are you a solicitor?' he asked, staring at me intently.

'Yes,' I replied.

'I'm extremely pleased to meet you,' said the old gentleman. 'Would you like to sit on this chair beside me?'

I thanked him, and sat with my notebook and pen at the ready. He gave his name, date of birth and his age, which was ninety-two.

'You look extremely well for ninety-two, sir,' I said politely.

'Well thank you, young man, I don't do badly really. The only problem I have is my legs. I can hear and I can see, but these wretched legs do let me down.'

I sympathised with him, pleased to talk to someone of his age with such mental agility. 'Do you like it here?' I asked.

'Yes, I do. I have a lovely room with a pleasant view over the gardens; I have books, and the staff are good enough to get me most of the daily papers, because I like to keep up with what's going on in the world. I'm only here because I can't get about and my family live away, in a flat, so I couldn't live with them, but they do visit me as often as they can. I'm well cared for, and fortunately I'm not a burden to anybody.'

I warmed to this friendly, articulate old man. We talked about a will, and I took his instructions, which were clear and concise. 'Who do you like best of the staff, then?' I asked him, trying to avoid ending the conversation too abruptly.

'They're all very good,' he said, 'but I suppose if I were to choose my favourite, I'd say it was Avril. She's got big tits!' he explained with a grin.

'Next client, please,' I said.

Another old gentleman came towards me and sat down. 'Do you want to make a will, sir?' I said.

There was no reply. I repeated it. No reply.

'I'm a solicitor, and I'm here to help people make a will.'

His stare moved across the room, then he stood and shouted 'Avril!' and walked off.

Next I was approached by an old lady, smartly dressed in a blue Paisley frock. Her snow-white hair was well-kept, and she had a bright, cheerful face.

'Hello,' I said.

'Beg your pardon?' she replied.

'I said hello, how are you?'

'Beg your pardon?' said the women.

'My name's Steve Smith, and I'm here to help people make wills.'

'You've come to help Will? What's the matter with Will, then?'

'Nothing's the matter with Will. I'm here about the will people prepare in case they die.'

'Has Will died?' she said, looking upset

'No, Will's not died, I'm not talking about…' I stopped talking when I noticed a hearing aid peering out of the top pocket of her cardigan. 'Would you like to turn that on?' I asked, pointing to the machine.

'Oh, it's a white cardie, I knitted it myself, that's what I've got on.'

Getting desperate, I said to her, 'Excuse me, I'll get help,' and fled.

By this time Roy had returned, having convinced the nurse that he was after all a visitor. She was extremely flustered and apologetic, and couldn't see the joke.

'That's all right, I suppose it was easily done, but I enjoyed the bed bath all the same,' he laughed.

I looked at him. 'You've not had a bed bath, have you?'

'Oh yes,' said Roy. 'Very nice too, I enjoyed it.' The nurse blushed and left the room.

My next client was a ninety-six-year-old, apparently the oldest resident. He had all his faculties, and told me that he took a long walk every day.

'How do you manage to keep so well?' I asked him.

'Roughage,' he said forcefully. 'Plenty of roughage.'

I didn't want to get into that discussion, so returned to the point of my visit, completed his instructions, and passed on to the next client, a well-dressed, young-looking and very mobile woman.

'Now then, my dear,' I said, 'would you like me to help you make a will?'

'Yes please,' she said, 'and while you're here, I'd love some advice.'

'Certainly madam,' I said. 'And how long have you been here?'

'Oh, about four years,' she said.

'Well, you look extremely well,' I said. Obviously it isn't polite for a man to ask a lady her age, but I was intrigued, so I plucked up the courage to say, 'Would you mind if I asked how old you are?'

'Not at all,' she said. 'I'm forty-seven.' She must have noted my confusion, because she added, 'I work here.'

'Oh, of course,' I replied, having nearly put both feet in it. 'And your name, madam?'

'Avril,' came the reply.

'Oh, Avril,' I said. 'I've been talking to one of your friends, the old gentleman in the wheelchair.'

'Oh, Colin,' she said. 'Yes, he's a right handful.'

'That's what he said about you,' I said.

By the time we'd finished, the tea gong had gone, and along came a tray of sandwiches and buns. I took a tea and a scone over to Don Juan. 'Here you are, sir,' I said.

'Thank you, young man. I saw you talking to Avril. Hasn't she got a big pair of…?'

I left rather quickly. As we jumped into the car, Wilf asked, 'Who volunteers to go back next week and get all the signatures?' No one replied.

Back at the office, Tracy told me a man called Sam had been in, and would call back just before we closed.

'Sam,' I said. 'It can't be Sam Trueman, he's in Majorca.'

But it was. He had a superb tan, looked very healthy, and it seemed that a few months in the warm sunshine had suited him.

'How are you, Sam?' I asked.

'I want you to buy my old house back, Steve,' he told me firmly.

'You're joking!' I said. 'We've only just managed to sell it. What in God's name is wrong?'

'I want to come home,' said Sam, almost tearfully. 'I can't stand the heat, it's so warm I can't go out. If I go in the pool, the chemicals give me a rash, I can't stand the food, and the people get on my wick. It's too hot to play football, and I'm lonely.'

I sat back in my chair and stared at him. 'You're a millionaire. You have everything you want, no worries, no stress, no problems whatsoever. All you have to do is enjoy life.'

'I can't do it there,' said Sam. 'I want to come home.' He handed me a bottle of Spanish brandy and said, 'You'll like this, it's a nice taste and doesn't give you indigestion.'

With that Wilf entered the room, having smelt alcohol, and was as surprised as me to see our sun-bronzed visitor. 'I'll have a glass of that,' he said, producing three glasses, and poured the brew. He sat with us as Sam explained the reason for his visit.

'It was all right at first,' said Sam. 'It was new and exciting, and I was really into it, if you know what I mean. I wanted for nothing, my meals were always ready on time, I had my choice of food, plenty of wine, sand, sun, sea and peace and quiet. But it was just too much. Too easy, too convenient. Oh, I know everybody dreams of such a life, but the time comes when you have to tell yourself the truth, and the truth in my case was that I didn't like it. If I could have moved it back to Rotherham and turned out with my pals when it suited me it would have been perfect, but I was away from everything and everyone I know, and it was too much of a culture shock.

'I don't doubt I've benefited from it in some way, if only that it's shown me where my real life is. I know you'll find it hard to understand, but if you'd been through it, I think you'd feel the same.'

I raised my eyebrows at Wilf, who silently signalled back his own astonishment. 'So what now, Sam?' I asked.

'I've worked everything out,' said Sam. 'I've arranged with some Spanish lawyers to give my housekeeper and her husband their bungalow and enough land around it so they can be self-sufficient if they want. The villa can be rented, and I'll get a bit of income off it and Isi and Toni will have a job looking after it. Then you can buy my house back. I want you to go to the new owners and tell them I want it back and don't care how much it costs. I sold it for £30,000, so offer them £35,000, or more if you have to. Whatever you do, just get it back for me.'

Wilf said, 'You're the client, Sam. If that's what you want, that's what we'll try to do.'

That very night, Wilf and I went to Sam's old house, now occupied by a young couple with a small baby. When we asked if they'd sell, the couple, not surprisingly, didn't want to know: they'd decorated it and settled in nicely, and didn't want the inconvenience of a further flit. We offered them £32,000, which meant £2,000 profit within a matter of months, but they weren't interested. They softened a little when we mentioned £35,000, and finally a deal was done at £37,500, with their legal fees and removal expenses thrown in.

There was a slight problem, as Sam wanted them out by the end of the month. But the young couple agreed to store their furniture at Sam's expense and move in with the girl's parents until a new home could be found. As it turned out, it wasn't long before they acquired semi-detached bungalow, and with their profit on the house transaction were able to move quite quickly. They were thrilled and so was Sam, and to us it was another job and another satisfied client.

A month later, Sam called to tell us that he'd got his old job back at the foundry. After that, I saw him quite regularly at football training sessions. I don't believe he ever returned to Majorca, but our photograph, taken outside the villa, was proudly displayed on his mantelpiece.

FIFTEEN

I FIND A CHEROKEE INDIAN
IN BELFAST

In the autumn of 1982 I embarked on one of my most interesting cases, the sort you'd be pleased to do for nothing. And apart from my expenses, I did just that.

Late one afternoon, after a long list of appointments, my last client for the day was a Mr Richard Pavey. I hadn't met him before, but I'd been recommended to him by a client I'd acted for some years previously.

Mr Pavey was a man of average height but striking facial characteristics, with a golden-brown skin. He introduced himself with a marked Welsh accent, but I was sure his origins were even further from Rotherham, although he was of no ethnic group that I could bring to mind. He explained that he had come to see me about his son Owen, who had been serving with the army in Northern Ireland until his death only a week before. Owen had been in the army for about three years of a nine-year engagement, and was stationed in Armagh in County Londonderry. He had been out on patrol, and on his return was shot by one of his own platoon. Unfortunately the Army had been somewhat tight-lipped about the circumstances, pending an inquiry, so Mr Pavey had come to me.

Because this was an unusual death, an inquest was to be held at the Armagh courthouse to establish, insofar as possible, exactly what had taken place. Mr Pavey Senior had a letter inviting him to the inquest and offering him transport to the courthouse. He told me he wanted an independent lawyer to represent him there, so that he could be confident of getting to the truth of the matter.

I explained that this case wouldn't attract legal aid, and although it was clear Mr Pavey had little or no funds, as he was living on unemployment benefit, he said he still wished to be represented at the hearing.

I believed that this was a case which required representation, so I told him that I would take it on, but he would have to pay all travelling and accommodation expenses, and he readily agreed. As there would be no documentation beforehand, the evidence being either given by witnesses or read out from statements at the inquest itself, I pointed out that we would need a 'noter' (someone who writes down the evidence as it is given), and Mr Pavey said he would meet the expense of that too, so I set about taking my instructions. I asked him if he thought there was anything sinister about what had happened, and he said he didn't know, but apparently the lad who had fired the gun was his son's best friend.

Understandably, Mr Pavey became upset as he told me the facts, and I thought I would help him regain his composure by talking about other things. Still intrigued by his appearance, I asked, 'I notice you have a Welsh accent, Mr Pavey. Is that where you're from originally?'

'I lived in South Wales just after the war, and stayed there for many years until I came to Yorkshire, but I'm actually Canadian by birth. I fought with the RAF during the war, and when it finished I settled in Wales.'

I still hadn't grasped what was unusual about the man, but there was definitely something different about him, so I asked where in Canada he was from. He gave me the area, and indeed named the town, but it meant nothing to me.

'I thought you didn't look Welsh,' I said, grappling for the words to ask the pertinent question.

'Oh, I understand what you mean,' he said. 'I'm actually a member of the Cherokee Tribe of American Indians.'

So that was it! I had indeed seen that look and skin colour before, but only in films.

'Surely Pavey is an unusual name for a Cherokee Indian?' I ventured.

'That's my adopted name,' he said, 'from the people I lived with in Wales. My real name's Richard Yellowknife.'

He explained that he had been born in Canada into the Cherokee tribe and brought up on a reservation before joining the forces. When he came to England he met a Welsh girl, and after the war they married and settled down. It was an unusual story, and in an attempt to take his mind off the case in hand, I persuaded him to tell me more about his youth and the tribe itself. We were getting on very well, and I phoned Tracy to organise some tea. As she brought it in, the sound of a trombone came from the landing.

'Have you got a musician on your staff?' Mr Pavey asked.

'Oh yes,' I replied. 'That's Oscar, he likes a blast now and again.'

We returned to business, and soon agreed that Mr Pavey, a 'noter' and I would fly to Belfast from Leeds on a date to be arranged. Having seen him out, I told Wilf about our new case, and explained that I would need a noter, but he turned me down flat.

'There are two reasons,' he said. 'First, we can't both be away for two days. And second, you're not getting me anywhere near Armagh. I might not get back.'

Wilf was referring to the massive media coverage of a day of violence less than a week before, when four people, including two policemen, had been shot dead. 'Let's face it,' he said, 'who are you going to persuade to fly to Belfast and then travel to Armagh to appear on behalf of a British soldier's family?'

'Well I suppose if you put it that way, I can see the problem. But I've promised him now,' I said. 'And besides, it's interesting.'

'It'll be interesting if you get bombed,' said Wilford.

'Well you can have all the debts, then,' I offered, and began thinking who might be prepared to go. I needed someone with nerves of steel and guts as wide as a bull's neck; a devil-may-care musketeer with a thirst for adventure. And I couldn't think of anyone who fitted that description.

That evening as I left to collect my car, I walked past Michael Jarvis's office. 'Yes!' I thought, and promptly hammered on his door.

'Now then, Smithy, what can I do for you?' said Jarvis.

'Well, a small gin wouldn't come amiss,' I said.

Jarvis produced a miniature bottle of Martell brandy and said that was the best he could do. 'The only other thing I can offer you is tea.'

'I'll have that, then,' I said, and when it arrived, promptly poured the brandy into it and set about drinking the invigorating brew.

'I'll tell you why I've called,' I said earnestly. 'I've been asked to represent a nice old boy whose son's been killed in the army in bizarre circumstances, and I'm desperate to help him get to the truth of his son's death. He's asked me to attend the inquest, but because I won't be able to see the evidence until the day itself, I need somebody to take notes for when I have to cross-examine the witnesses. It involves a pleasant flight and one night and a couple of days away, all expenses paid. What do you say?'

'Marvellous idea,' said Jarvis, 'I'd be delighted to come with you. Where is it?'

I had dreaded that question, but at least I'd already got his agreement. 'Oh, in Ireland,' I said casually.

'Ireland,' said Jarvis suspiciously. 'Where in Ireland?'

'Armagh,' I said, waiting for the explosion. In the split second that preceded his answer I imagined various replies, all ending in 'off', but to my surprise Jarvis announced, 'I've always wanted to go to Northern Ireland. Count me in.'

I left before he could have second thoughts, promising to let him have the date of the trip as soon as possible. Three or four days later, Mr Pavey rang to say the inquest had been fixed for a fortnight hence, and his son's unit commander had offered accommodation for all three of us. More importantly, a driver would collect us from Belfast airport, which would save us a great deal of time and effort. Meanwhile I had written to the army, telling them of my interest in the case, and their reply was very helpful.

When Mr Pavey came in to finalise the arrangements, he seemed withdrawn, and I asked him what the problem was.

'Well you see, there's been a lot of publicity about my son's case, and your name's been mentioned in the papers as being my solicitor.'

'I saw it, but I'm not worried about that. A bit of publicity doesn't trouble me.'

'It's not that,' said Mr Pavey. 'I don't quite know how to tell you this, but you ought to know. Someone claiming to be the IRA has written to me, saying that when we get to Ireland, we'll be seen to.'

'Seen to?' I queried anxiously, alarm bells ringing in both ears.

'Yes, seen to,' said Mr Pavey. 'I suppose they do it to everybody just to intimidate them, but I wouldn't blame you if you told me you didn't want to go.'

I had discussed the case with a number of friends and colleagues, and what would they think of me if I dropped out because of a threat? And the headlines would be really inspiring … ROTHERHAM SOLICITOR GETS COLD FEET, or ROTHERHAM SOLICITOR BACKS OUT OF COURT CASE, or even worse, ROTHERHAM SOLICITOR DONE BY INTIMIDATION. So I convinced myself he was right and the threat wasn't genuine, took a deep breath, and told my client that it didn't make any difference to me. But I must admit I was relieved when he told me the Army would collect us from the VIP lounge at Belfast airport in one of their armoured personnel carriers.

I decided not to trouble Jarvis with the mention of the threatening letter. When the day arrived, I collected him and drove to Leeds, where we parked the car and went into the airport lounge to meet Mr Pavey – or Dick, since we were on first-name terms by now – for the 7.30am flight. He and Jarvis hit it off immediately, and on the plane, Dick treated us to a drink. I suppose it was a little early, but it was part of the trip, so we each had a large brandy with our coffee – I because I was nervous, and Jarvis because he liked it.

Within an hour, we were circling above Belfast. Dick turned to Jarvis and said, 'You're both very brave men, and I thank you.'

'Oh, we're used to flying,' said Jarvis. 'It doesn't bother us at all.'

'I don't mean flying,' said Dick. 'I mean coming to Northern Ireland when there's all this trouble….'

'Oh, that's all right,' said Jarvis. 'Lots of people visit Belfast and never see any trouble.'

This was only days after the IRA had killed eleven soldiers and four young women in a pub bombing. I was beginning to feel proud of Jarvis, but I fervently hoped that would be the end of it. But Dick continued innocently, '…particularly in view of that letter.'

I was done for. Jarvis was on to it like a flash. 'What letter?' he asked in a disturbed tone.

'The one from the IRA,' said Dick, 'about us being blown up when we get here.'

Jarvis looked at me and said through gritted teeth, 'You didn't tell me anything about this.'

'I forgot,' I said lamely, then, more confidently, 'At least we've got the Army to look after us. I've never been in an armoured personnel carrier before.'

'Do they carry coffins?' said Jarvis.

In the VIP lounge, we were approached by a man in jeans and T-shirt, who was distinctive only by his short-cropped hair. He looked every inch a soldier in civilian clothes.

'Mr Pavey, Mr Smith and colleague?' he asked, referring to a sheet of paper. 'I'm Lance Corporal Johnson, here to take you to Omagh.'

'We're not going to Omagh,' I said. 'We're going to Armagh.'

'Not according to my orders,' he said. 'I was told to collect three gentlemen and take them to Omagh.'

'No, we're definitely going to Armagh,' Dick said. 'I arranged everything with Sergeant McCloud,' and I chipped in with the reason for our visit.

'I don't think I can go to Armagh,' said the Lance Corporal. 'I don't have a weapon. We have to be issued weapons if we're going into that area. I'd better contact base.'

He returned after two or three minutes to tell us that he had to take us to Armagh barracks, and led us out to the car park.

'Where's your armoured car?' asked Jarvis.

'Over there,' said the soldier, pointing to an old red Cortina. My heart sank. Someone, somewhere, had made a mistake.

'We thought we were being collected in an armoured staff car,' I said.

'I don't know anything about that,' said the soldier. 'Besides, they do tend to stand out a little.'

'Do you mean we're better off travelling incognito, as it were?'

'Doesn't really matter. British Army cars are a dead giveaway, because they have seatbelts in the back.'

We spent the next half hour asking the soldier a number of questions about the area in general and Armagh in particular. 'Armagh's not a very safe place, certainly not for us Brits,' was pretty much all his answers amounted to. 'Bloody marvellous,' I thought.

Travelling through Belfast, I wasn't impressed with what I saw – though in fairness, it was an overcast day, which wouldn't endear any town to a visitor. As we reached open countryside, I saw a dead cow lying on its back at the side of the road. Rigor mortis had set in, and its legs were pointed upwards. 'Looks as though that's a dead cow,' I said, hoping for an explanation.

'Yes,' said the soldier, 'seems dead, all right.'

I looked at Jarvis, who looked back at me with a stare that said, 'Why have you got me into this?'

The journey was uneventful until we took a wrong turning and arrived in a rather downbeat area where pedestrians leered into the car as though they knew who we were. The soldier realised that we'd gone astray, and I noticed a hint of panic in his voice when he said so. Just then we approached a sign which said 'Crossmaglen', and he performed the quickest three-point turn I've ever experienced and attempted to retrace our journey. We eventually got across the boundary to Armagh and I breathed a sigh of relief. Lance Corporal Johnson said, 'I'll ask for directions.' I hoped he wouldn't ask one of the locals, because I wasn't sure what would result, but we soon came across a group of Royal Ulster Constabulary officers at a checkpoint. Our driver pulled up beside them, and an officer came towards the car with his automatic rifle cocked.

'Bloody marvellous again,' I thought, with even more concern. But our driver immediately announced who he was, and his cockney accent appeared to relax the policeman. We were given directions, and set off for what we hoped would be Armagh Barracks. But whenever we stopped at traffic lights, I still had the impression that passers-by were staring into the car. It was an unnerving experience, made worse by the fact that our driver was clearly terrified as well.

We then spotted in the distance a large building with a castle-like appearance. 'That'll be it,' said the lance corporal, breathing a sigh of relief.

We drove up to the gates, which opened, and at the checkpoint found that we weren't in the barracks but in Armagh prison, the home of H Block itself. We were allowed to turn our vehicle round, and directed further up the hill to another castle-like building, which we were assured was the British Army barracks. I've never been more pleased to see soldiers on guard duty.

We drove in, had our identities checked, and were shown into the reception area. I winked at Jarvis, and said, 'Piece of cake.'

'Piece of shit,' he replied, and I laughed.

Our host, Sergeant McCloud, soon came to greet us. We were shown to our quarters, and after a superb lunch in the Sergeants' Mess, our car to the courthouse arrived.

The courthouse was only minutes away, but during the journey we heard our case referred to in some detail on the radio news. It had clearly caused a lot of local interest, and indeed, television cameras and a number of photographers were outside the building.

Inside, I was approached by a gentleman who looked like a court usher, wearing long black robes, who introduced himself with a title I couldn't quite catch and said the coroner wanted to see me in his chambers before the case started. Jarvis and I followed him along a warren of corridors to a room marked 'Coroner'. At his knock a voice from within shouted 'Enter', and we were admitted to a large room with a huge leather-topped desk in the centre. The walls were adorned with paintings of what appeared to be our host's predecessors, and in the corner, hanging on a large oak contraption, was a gown and wig.

The coroner introduced himself and shook hands with us both. He politely explained the procedure he liked in his court, then enquired how long we would be staying in Northern Ireland. We said just overnight, but he said that since there had been a lot of publicity surrounding this case, it would be in our best interests to leave as soon as possible. I thanked him, and went into the court, which was very traditional, with marble-floored corridors leading to oak-panelled courtrooms with brass-railed docks, and the smell of brass polish lingering in the cool air.

I introduced myself to the advocate, who was there to give the facts to the coroner and call the evidence, and he was kind enough to give me an outline of the case. The evidence to be called included the soldier who had fired the weapon, another soldier who was present when the incident occurred, and the pathologist who had done the autopsy. There were other witness statements which merely set the scene and were not contentious, so could be agreed without the presentation of oral evidence.

The first witness to give evidence was the soldier who had actually pulled the trigger, Owen Pavey's best friend. His voice trembled as he took the oath, but the coroner reassured him and asked him to answer the questions as clearly and audibly as he could. He was asked his name, rank and serial number before recounting the events of the day in question.

He explained that they had been on a five-man patrol in Armagh. There was a lot of tension in the city at the time, and the squad had been particularly alert for trouble. When they returned to the barracks, they went to the gunroom to discharge their weapons. He said he had been holding his rifle in a cradle-like position, waiting his turn, chatting with Pavey to his right, when, in the soldier's own words, 'I must have had my finger on the trigger, and the gun just went off.'

He was asked if he had had any intention to shoot, and said not. He was then asked if there had been any messing about, and denied that as well, but seemed discomposed by the question. The advocate left it at that, and I was given the option to cross-examine.

It was important for me to show that there had been negligence on the part of this soldier, because this would affect Mr Pavey's right to compensation. Under the Crown Proceedings Act, a soldier's family isn't entitled to compensation for the loss of their loved one on active duty, although they are usually given some allowances, and sometimes a pension. In certain cases ex gratia payments are made, and if we could show that Owen's death was caused by someone else's negligence, the Army might be more disposed towards that option. I therefore had to cross-examine this man with a view to getting him to accept that he had behaved negligently, and was thus responsible for Owen's death. It wasn't going to be pleasant for the lad, nor for me.

I first told him there was no suggestion of intent about his actions, to which he merely nodded: I don't think such a proposition had ever entered his mind. Then I asked one or two general questions about the patrol, before turning to the normal procedure in the gunroom, which he explained quite confidently. Next, I simply asked:

'Why didn't you have your safety catch on?'

The soldier thought for a second, then, realising that there was little point in trying to conceal the truth, simply answered, 'I forgot.'

'And if the safety catch had been on, the gun wouldn't have gone off?'

Without equivocation, he answered, 'No, and Owen wouldn't be dead.' His head sank forward in distress.

I asked no further questions. There was silence for a second or two before the coroner announced that he had no further questions either, and the soldier was allowed to leave the witness box. As he walked past the solicitors' bench, he looked at me briefly with relief written on his face. I looked at Jarvis for a reaction, and he simply shrugged. It had been no sparkling act of cross-examination, since the soldier had never meant to be dishonest; it was almost as if he were clearing his conscience. From that point of view it was the easiest case I've ever dealt with, but in another way it was perhaps the most difficult.

The next witness was a member of the patrol who confirmed what the first witness had said. Although he did his best to help his friend, he had to concede that if the safety catch had been on, the gun wouldn't have gone off. Another witness followed in similar vein, before the pathologist gave unchallenged evidence about the cause of death. Fortunately, Owen would not have suffered, as we were told his death would have been instantaneous.

I briefly summed up my case to the coroner, complimenting the soldiers on their honesty and suggesting that this was one of those awful quirks of fate which had resulted in tragedy. I found myself actually mitigating the matter so far as the unfortunate soldier was concerned. All I had to prove was that there was some degree of negligence, as was clearly accepted by the soldier himself and the other witnesses. The coroner retired for a short time before returning and announcing an open verdict. I looked towards Dick, who was sitting behind me, but his face displayed no reaction.

As we left the courtroom, the advocate for the coroner came up to me and shook my hand, saying, 'Well done, you should be home and dry now on an ex gratia payment.' I thanked him, pointing out that I hadn't really done anything but ask the obvious question.

Outside, the soldier was waiting. He just said, 'Mr Pavey…', unable to complete his sentence.

Dick couldn't speak either, but words weren't really necessary. The two men shook hands and embraced each other. Jarvis and I discreetly left them to find our driver. After two minutes or so, Dick and the soldier came into view. There was an exchange of glances, then the soldier was gone, with one of his friends' arms consolingly around him.

No one spoke in the car, and at the barracks we went to our own rooms for half an hour before going down for dinner. Jarvis and I decided not to stay overnight, although Dick did. Sergeant McCloud kindly provided transport, and we set off for Belfast airport. The car radio was on, and the news referred to the inquest, reporting the 'sensational disclosures uncovered by the deceased's family's solicitor'. It made no reference to a soldier who had lost his best friend, ruined his own career, and possibly his life, by telling the truth. Three months later, Owen Pavey's estate was awarded an ex gratia payment. I never enquired after Owen's friend, since I thought he might prefer it that way.

SIXTEEN

CHIMP CHAOS AND
MRS MOTT'S KIDS

By autumn 1982 Wilford Smith & Co. were thriving, despite the deepening recession and record unemployment, and on the point of taking on two more staff to cope with the ever-increasing workload. Wilf and I had everything we could wish for – indeed, we felt we were the luckiest men alive. But we were also actively looking for new premises to cope with our expansion, which wasn't proving easy.

Our friends were a 'Dream Team', who would do anything to help each other. Michael Jarvis looked after the accounts, and did his best to stop us plundering our reserves. Lewis Frame, the 'Mad Scotsman' from the Leeds Permanent Building Society, helped us with conveyancing, as did Timbo Johnson from the Bradford and Bingley and his mate Fred from Eagle Star. Keith Copley, the principal clerk from the magistrates clerks' office, was a bar-room pal with whom I shared many a joke in the courtrooms of Rotherham, and Bodger Broom could be trusted to appear with his hammer whenever his services were required. And of course there was Sean Page, who would just appear, and drive us to distraction with his schizophrenic humour. Some of our best times were when the gang got together for our monthly soirées, which were also often attended by four other good friends – Tenbelly Norburn, Chris Good, Don Morton and the Hemingfield Fusilier Tom Furness.

One day, browsing through the junk mail, I spotted an impressively embossed invitation to a variety show at the Rotherham Civic Theatre. The programme included a number of entertainers who had been plugging away at their trade for many years in the Micawberish belief that something would turn up, including one Rik Romola, a magician, and his chimpanzee assistant, Mitch. Rik had long since given up any idea of hitting the big time, and his disillusionment seemed to have rubbed off on Mitch, who was ill-mannered and aggressive. Rik only got work because he was cheap, and one of a dwindling number of novelty acts that could fill a gap between a singer and a comedian.

I got in touch with the gang and suggested we start our evening out at the Civic Theatre. Everyone agreed, and Sean Page was particularly keen.

'Oh, well done,' he enthused, 'I've got a pal on the show, Max. He's a comic; with a name like Crapper, I expected him to use a stage name, but he didn't... I'll take you and the gang to meet him for a drink at the interval – he's so nervous he can't go on unless he's pissed.'

I should have known better: the stage, alcohol and Page made a recipe for disaster. But it sounded like a good idea at the time...

He arrived late, just as the curtain was going up, and staggered along the line of seats, standing on people's feet and falling into a number of laps along the way. As we were in the fifth row of the stalls, he managed to disturb most of the audience, and by the time he finally joined us the first act, a dancer, had finished without many of us seeing a step. But in the bar at the interval, as promised, he introduced us to Max.

Max was to be the last act of the evening, whose job was to send the audience home with smiles on their faces, and he certainly looked nervous. But when he spotted Page approaching, his expression changed from apprehension to blind terror: he made some excuse, and left us to get our own drinks.

Page then produced a bar of laxative chocolate he'd 'borrowed' from his mum, who worked in a nursing home. 'Fancy a piece?' he asked.

'No thanks,' said Jarvis. 'Try Norburn, his need's greater than mine.'

'Put it away, Sean!' I said. 'That could do some damage.'

'Certainly could,' said Page. 'We'll have to try it out on someone later.'

Just then Rik came in, with Mitch on his shoulder, the chimp spitting at people as they walked past. But it made the mistake of its life when it tugged Pagey's ear.

'I say, steady on!' said Page.

'It was your own fault,' said Rik. 'You must've upset him.'

'Upset him? There ought to be a muzzle on it,' said Page, as the nasty creature pulled his hair.

Rik moved on, but not before Mitch had pulled a wax grape from the Lady Mayoress's hat and, as if he knew Pagey had been complaining about him, threw it, hitting him on the back of the head. That was the moment war was declared.

While Rik went to the bar for a drink, Mitch sat on a chair near our group. Pagey took the laxative chocolate out of his pocket, looked at it and then at the chimp. Mitch looked at the chocolate and then at Pagey.

Page walked towards Mitch, who bared his teeth. Page bared his teeth back, and Mitch looked really frightened. Having established his superiority, Page held out a piece of chocolate. The chimp snatched it and rammed it into his mouth, chewing vigorously.

Page broke off another piece and handed it to the greedy chimp; in a gulp, that too had gone. I was about to intervene when Mitch snatched the rest of the bar and I gobbled it down.

Page turned to me with a broad grin. 'That'll teach the bastard,' he said. 'That ape'll fart for England when that stuff gets hold. It works on the old folks in fifteen minutes, so Christ knows what it'll do to a bloody monkey,' he ended triumphantly.

Just then the three-minute bell rang, so we finished our drinks and went back to our seats. Rik Romola was the penultimate act. The master of ceremonies, an old stager with false teeth that clicked when he spoke, introduced him, and on danced Rik to a souped-up version of 'Tea For Two', packs of cards falling from his sleeves. Then, much to the delight of the children in the audience, he produced Mitch as if from nowhere.

It was clear the animal was already in some discomfort, and the microphone picked up the odd fart. There was some giggling and whispering among the younger members of the audience, then Pagey stood up and shouted, 'I do believe that monkey's farting in time with the music!'

The whole audience started laughing. Mitch began pulling cards out of Rik's breast pocket, for which he received rapturous applause. Then, as he leaned over to get a monkey nut as a reward for his trick, the audience discovered the power of laxative chocolate – the left side of Rik's white suit was doused in liquid chimpanzee excrement.

The shocked silence only lasted a second before laughter rolled round the theatre once more, and as Mitch switched shoulders to snatch a bunch of flowers that had magically appeared, the right-hand side of Rik's suit acquired a stain to match the left. With classic timing, two white doves appeared and settled on Rik's outstretched hands just as Mitch released the biggest fart of the evening, accompanied by another very moist bowel movement. Two piebald doves flew to sanctuary offstage as Rik made his bow.

The guffaws were still echoing round the hall when the MC came on to introduce the last act. He waited for them to die down, then took a deep breath before announcing, 'And now, ladies and gentlemen, to send you home with a smile on your face, our very own cheeky chappy, Max Crapper!'

At that point, the lungful of stink he'd inhaled got to him, and he just managed to turn away from the microphone before vomiting with such force that his false teeth shot across the stage. Max, making his entrance on cue, saw a pair of teeth smiling up at him. Sidestepping, he slipped on a patch of Mitch's offerings, skidded across the stage right into the MC, and fell heavily backwards, hitting his head hard on the floor. But as he drifted into unconsciousness, I'm sure he heard the audience clapping, stamping their feet and chanting, 'We want Max Crapper! We want Max Crapper…!'

The stage manager, belatedly realising something had gone wrong, brought down the curtain and put the house lights on, and as the audience made our way out, the talk was of nothing else. Pagey, with a wicked glint in his eye and obviously feeling not a twinge of guilt, said, 'When I saw the programme I thought Max Crapper was another act, not just a description of Rik's assistant.'

The following day, feeling a little worse for wear, I was opening the post when I was accosted by Mrs Mott, the cleaner we had employed a year before.

'Our Martin loves that job,' she said, a cigarette dangling precariously from her mouth. ''E's never late, 'e's even early… 'E'll work overtime when 'e can get it… Aye, 'e's a good lad, our Martin.'

When Mrs Mott was determined to talk, there was no stopping her. 'You busy, then, Mr Smith?' she asked, not really caring about the reply.

'Yes,' I replied, in the certain knowledge that my answer wouldn't deter her. 'Very busy, and I really should get stuck in straight away.'

'Aye,' countered Mrs Mott, 'I can always tell when you're busy. You squint with your eyes. It's like vomit,' she elaborated.

'What is?' I asked, somewhat confused.

'Work. When it's got to be done, it's got to be done. Aye, that's our Martin,' she said. 'Work, work, work, in'it? Aye, 'e loves that job, our Martin. Loves it.'

She wanted me to ask, and wouldn't go until I did. 'All right,' I said, 'what does he do?'

Mrs Mott inhaled, coughed, and after a pause said, ''E kills pigs. For the abattoir. Kills 'em dead.' To underline the point, she drew her thumb across her throat.

Despite her annoying talkativeness, there was something endearing about Mrs Mott. She hadn't enjoyed much in her life, except for the five children who were her pride and joy. Her marriage had foundered after twenty-five years, and thirteen years later she still missed her husband. A once-pretty woman, worn by stress, her honest face was still illuminated by striking emerald-green eyes, and she'd kept both her figure and her dignity. She was also one of the most hard-working and loyal women I ever met, so we just had to put up with her less desirable traits.

'Now our Malcolm, 'e's another good worker,' she continued. 'We call him Talcum, 'cos of where he works. Sewerage works!' she continued triumphantly. ''E shovels…'

Before she could finish, I invited her to make some tea. It arrived minus sugar. I always have sugar in my tea, except when Mrs Mott makes it.

'I've not put sugar in, Mr Smith. No wonder you're carrying all that weight. You want to use sweeteners; they're the best thing, are sweeteners. All my lads use 'em.'

'Well I'll stick to sugar,' I said. When she returned with it I thanked her, to be told, 'I can't stand here talking to you all day, I've got work to do.'

I then heard the sound of someone tripping over the Hoover on the landing, followed by much swearing. Wilf had arrived.

He sat down heavily, his face grey and his eyes puffed up. 'I must have eaten something dodgy last night,' he said, in an attempt to explain away a massive hangover. I left him with a large mug of tea and three Anadins before setting off for Rotherham Magistrates' Court.

As I walked up the steps, a group of Asian gentlemen huddled in conversation at the top stopped talking, and a broad Yorkshire accent called, 'Eh up, tha's Steve Smith, aren't tha?'

I turned to their spokesman, who was about twenty, and wearing a large white frock-type garment and a strange hat. He beamed at me, and told me that his brother was in the cells. 'It's our Tariq, tha knows, 'e's locked up, and we want thee to represent 'im, if tha sees what I mean, like.'

I would have loved to reply in Punjabi, but unfortunately couldn't. The lad introduced me to his father, uncle, brother, cousin, stepbrother, the local holy man, and an interpreter, and the supporters' club followed me into the courtroom, where I found them places so they could follow the proceedings.

My morning visits to the cells were always delightful experiences. The last time any of the walls saw a lick of paint would have been at the time of the Coronation – probably Edward VII's. The newly appointed jailer was PC Kemp, an old stager with over thirty years' experience and a great deal of integrity. 'Aw reet, love,' he said, 'who does tha want to see?'

I gave him the list of three prisoners, and he promptly brought out someone I'd never seen before who wasn't on the list. 'I don't act for this man, Derek,' I said.

'Aw reet, love, who does tha want, then?'

'How about one of those on the list I gave you?' I said.

'OK love,' answered PC Kemp, failing to notice my sarcasm, and brought out Tariq.

Tariq was about nineteen, short, with jet-black hair and suspiciously roving eyes. He handed me his charge sheet, and I read that the police were alleging he had taken three vehicles without consent. Unfortunately the last one had been chased by the police and involved in a crash. I noted a wound to his forehead, which had been stitched, and there was some blood staining his colourful shirt.

He explained that he'd gone out with two white youths, who lived near him, and they'd decided to steal a car. Tariq didn't want to, but succumbed to peer pressure because he was afraid he'd be ostracised if he didn't. He said that he'd simply got into the car after the other two lads had taken it. His father was furious, as they were a hard-working and law-abiding family, and it was hard for him to accept the shame his son had brought upon their house. His father represented the old ways, in which children were expected to keep out of trouble and respect their elders, but the new generation of Asians growing up in Britain found it difficult to live by customs laid down many centuries ago in a country they'd never seen.

Unfortunately Tariq had no option but to plead guilty, which meant he would acquire a criminal record and upset his family even more. It was my job to try to keep the penalty to the minimum. I suspected the real punishment would be inflicted on Tariq when he left court, a point I decided to put to the bench before they came to their own conclusions.

My next client was an unsavoury-looking gentleman from the biking fraternity. His leather jacket and filthy denim jeans could have walked in on their own; his long, straggly hair had probably last seen a shower when he walked through a cloudburst; and his tangled beard seemed to stretch up to his eye sockets. His eyebrows were in a similar state, and he spoke with a growl, as if perpetually trying to clear his throat. There was a heavy smell of Petulia oil about him, used by many to cover up the smell of cannabis.

He sat down and produced two charge sheets, which looked as though they had been rolled in oil and gravy. I opened them with my fingertips, to find that he had been charged with GBH.

'If you think I'm pleading guilty to these you can kiss my arse,' he said defiantly as I looked up.

'No thanks, I'd rather not. Tell me what happened.'

'I was minding me own business when this effin' landlord came up and suggested that I was smoking cannabis. I said "Knackers" and 'e took offence. 'E told me to leave, and I refused because I 'adn't finished me pint and I wasn't putting up with 'is manner. 'E reached down to take 'old of me arm, and nobody touches me, so I cracked 'im.'

'Well that makes you guilty of assault, doesn't it?' I asked.

'Fuck off,' said the biker indignantly. 'I were defending mesen. 'E touched me, so I touched 'im.'

'Yes, but he touched your arm with his fingers, and you hit him in the teeth with your fist. According to this charge sheet, you knocked three of them out. What's the assault on the police officer about?'

'Well, I left the pub, see, and as I were walking down the road to me bike, a squad car came screaming up, this young copper jumped out and took 'old of me arm, and nobody does that, so I...'

'Cracked him?' I interposed. 'Self-defence, I suppose.'

'Right,' said the biker. 'I want out, man. I want me freedom, I want me rights, I want something to eat, and I want me cigs.'

'Anything else?' I asked. 'A hacksaw, or a shower perhaps?'

'Look,' he snarled, 'I don't take kindly to cells, I don't take kindly to coppers, and I don't take kindly to people who touch me. I don't like being touched.'

I sighed. 'Well, first I'll sort out the question of bail, and then we'll talk about whether you're guilty or not.'

'OK man, stay cool,' said the biker, who was clearly unable to take his own advice.

My third prisoner was a lady who hadn't paid her fine for failure to possess a television licence. She tearfully explained that her husband had given her the money for the licence, but she'd spent it on food. She was clearly afraid of him, and it seemed he knew nothing about the court appearance, so I agreed to get her case called on first so she could get home and possibly avoid her husband's wrath.

As I was about to leave the cells, PC Kemp called me back. 'Steve, love, there's another for you, just brought in. Drunk and disorderly, criminal damage, urinating in a public place and – oh yes, theft. I'll bring him in.'

I went back into the interview room and got my papers out in readiness. The door opened, and a lad of about seventeen walked in. He had curly blond hair and a bright, clean complexion, apart from a massive lump over his left eye surrounded by heavy fresh bruising. The other eye was clear, and an unusual emerald-green colour. He was wearing a bloodstained white shirt and jeans, and looked embarrassed and sorry for himself.

'Sit down, young man,' I said, 'and give me your sheets.'

I looked at the charge sheets and read, 'Michael Morris...' My voice tailed off as I saw the surname: Mott.

I was silent for a second or two, trying to decide whether or not to express recognition, as I didn't wish to embarrass him. Fortunately, he took the decision from me. 'You're Steve Smith, aren't you?' he said. 'My mum's your cleaner.'

'Oh?' I said, feigning surprise. 'I hadn't realised that.'

'Aye, and she'll kill me if she knows where I am, but when the jailer asked if I knew a solicitor your name was the only one I could think of.'

I immediately put his mind at rest. 'Don't worry, Michael, I won't say anything to your mum.'

'Thank God,' he said fervently. 'She'd kill me.'

I asked him to tell his story, and while he did so checked the history the jailer had given to me, which described him as a seventeen-year-old, employed, with no previous convictions.

He explained that he and some friends had been at a party, where there had been a competition to drink the party cocktail in one go. It had clearly been a lethal concoction, and Michael had tried it repeatedly.

'I can't really remember what happened,' said Michael, 'but my mates damaged a car, took something out of it and threw it at me. Someone shouted, "Run!" and the next thing I remember was trying to run down the street. After a few yards I had to stop because I was busting for a wee. I stood in a doorway and had just started when a bobby grabbed me. He was getting piss all down my trousers, so I pushed him in the chest to get clear. Next thing I knew I was in the police station.'

'How did you get the black eye?' I asked.

Head bowed, he explained the officer had hit him in the face.

'Why?' I asked.

'I suppose I asked for it,' said Master Mott. 'After all, I'd pushed him. Look, Mr Smith, if me mum gets to know about this, my feet won't touch the floor. All I want to do is get it sorted and out of here. You'll never see me back in court again, I've learnt my lesson. I'm not bothered what they do to me, so long as they don't tell me mum.'

His attitude was refreshing, after so many lads who only worried about themselves and cared nothing for the well-being of others. This lad had behaved out of character with a group who had led him astray. With a fair wind and a good bench, I thought I might be able to cut him a deal, or 'weigh him off', as solicitors call it.

Unfortunately, it wasn't a good bench. I'd landed the Honourable Lord Chief Justice, my least-favourite magistrate. He didn't like me, I didn't like him, and we each knew how the other felt. The Lord Chief would want an adjournment for probation reports, which would mean a visit by a probation officer to Michael's home, which in turn would embarrass Mrs Mott so much that I believed she wouldn't be able to continue working for us, her pride damaged beyond recovery. I decided to call the biker first, to allow the Lord Chief to vent his spleen on the 'bad guy', in the hope that when Michael's case came on he'd have the punishment factor out of his system.

The biker walked into court demonstrating a marked reluctance to show any respect at all, which sealed his fate from the start. Whatever I thought of the Lord Chief, he was entitled to respect for his office, but didn't get any from my recalcitrant client. I used every point I could to secure bail, and when the bench retired my client beckoned me to the dock. I walked over expecting some appreciation of what I thought had been a masterly plea, but was greeted in a different vein.

'Tha didn't tell 'em me girlfriend's pregnant,' the lout complained.

'You didn't tell me,' I pointed out. 'Anyway, so what?'

Surprised at my reaction, 'So what?' he said. ''S' obvious, in't it, she needs me.'

'I don't think the fact you've dropped some bird in the club is going to make any difference to whether this bench grants you bail or not. I think they'll say if you'd thought about the girl you wouldn't have got into trouble in the first place,' I said.

'But I've got to be out to look after her,' protested the biker. 'Anyway, whose side are you on?'

'Yours, which is why I'm not coming out with complete bollocks to the court,' I said, putting it in language he might understand.

'If I don't get bail, I'm kicking off,' he announced, at which the court sergeant, who was standing nearby, radioed downstairs for reinforcements. Soon the dock contained not only my client and his guard, but three other large police officers with a collective weight of almost eighty stone.

When the magistrates returned and announced that they were

remanding my client in custody for fear that he would commit further offences, the biker rose and issued a vitriolic complaint, which included the phrase, 'You fuckin' thick bastard, tha ought to be shot wi shit!' Then the fun really stared. He refused to leave the dock, whereupon four burly officers enthusiastically manhandled him towards the door behind which was the spiral staircase to the cell area. Once the door was closed, the clattering sounds of a man falling downstairs were heard, followed by a voice tailing off into the distance: 'Oh my goodness, I hope you aren't hurt…'

The court sergeant returned adjusting his tie, and told me my client wanted to see me as soon as he'd been brought back from hospital.

Young Mott was next up, and presented an entirely different picture. With his head bowed he entered a guilty plea, and the prosecutor, an old friend of mine called John Brind, opened his case. (John was a good prosecutor and also an excellent musician, and we spent much of our time talking about music when we should have been discussing cases.)

I suggested the magistrate would need a report from a probation officer before Michael's case could be dealt with, anticipating that he would do the opposite to anything I recommended. Sure enough, he ran true to character.

'No, I don't think so, Mr Smith. This is clearly a case we can deal with today,' he said, smiling smugly.

I gracefully yielded, and proceeded to mitigate the case, pointing out what a good lad and hard worker he was, and every other point I could think of, before listening to the magistrate fine him £100. I saw Michael in the cells before he left, and his only worry was where the fine notice would be sent, because his mother always opened his mail. I told him I would collect it myself, and he could fetch it from my office at the end of the week and make his payments directly to the court.

Back in court, I saw with horror a reporter from the *Rotherham*

Advertiser copying the list of charges from the court list. Before I could say anything, he'd gone, armed with enough information to castigate the unfortunates who had appeared that day in Friday's edition. I considered asking him not to print Michael Mott's story, but thought that might just draw attention to it, so kept it to myself and hoped for the best.

On Friday morning, when I went into the office, the *Rotherham Advertiser* was on the reception counter, and Mrs Mott busy with her Hoover only a few feet away. I picked it up and took it into my office: this was one paper she wasn't going to see that morning.

I scanned each page for any reference to the case, and my heart sank when on page seven I saw the sub-headline DRUNKEN YOB STEALS FROM CAR. It would be only a matter of time before Mrs Mott got to know, unless I did something about it: she usually took the paper home after work on Mondays. So I tore out page seven, screwed it up, and was about to throw it in the bin when a photograph of a monkey caught my eye. It was Mitch, and the headline read MITCH SAVED FROM DEATH ROW.

I straightened out the paper and read that Max Crapper, the well-known local comedian, had received a serious head wound in an accident at the Civic Theatre after, as the police believed, he had been attacked by a performing chimpanzee. The chimp was known to be aggressive, and had been unwell on the night in question; moreover, a piece of tooth had been found embedded in Max's skull. With all this evidence against the chimp, the police ordered Rik to have him put down.

However, when Rik took Mitch to the vet for the lethal injection, the vet checked Mitch's teeth and found no recently broken ones. In the face of his expert opinion, the police asked a forensic expert to examine the piece of tooth taken from Max's skull. The result surprised everyone. Max's head had been viciously gnawed by a pair of false teeth.

Mitch was reprieved, but in view of what had happened Rik decided to retire him to a monkey sanctuary in the south of England, as suggested by the RSPCA, who had visited him in response to an anonymous phone call implying Mitch had been ill-treated during the show. I sensed Page's involvement in this.

Once again, I screwed up the page and threw it in the bin, put the paper on top of the fish tank and got on with my work. Alongside Mitch's drama, the story of a drunken young man's stupidity would be long dead by Monday.

SEVENTEEN

SHE MAY BE UGLY, BUT JANE CAN'T HALF FEIGHT

When Wilf and I set up in business together, the thought of having too many clients never entered our heads, but eighteen months later I was beginning to realise that a successful practice can be a nightmare. Being in two places at once had been written into my job description, sleep was becoming a luxury, and as for home life… My family were very tolerant, but I wish I'd known then what I do now – that it's often the people who matter most who get the least of one's time and attention.

What made it worthwhile was the knowledge that once in a while, among the mass of routine cases there would be that special one. Many factors can make a case special – it could be the personality of the client, the nature of the crime, or an unusual point of law. But one category of crime is always special. For the aficionado, there's no case quite like murder.

One bright October morning, having spent most of the night in Maltby police station helping an ungrateful client, I arrived late at the office at 9.15am knowing it was going to be a bad day, and fated to get worse as fatigue set in. I'd promised to dictate a brief to counsel and deliver it to the barrister's chambers by 10am, but couldn't find the file, and my Dictaphone appeared to have buggered off somewhere.

'Who's got my bloody Dictaphone?' I shouted down the corridor. There was no answer.

'Is everybody dead?' I demanded. Obviously they were, because no one answered, at least not until Mrs Mott peered around my door.

'Morning, Mr Smith. You're late this morning – one too many last night, eh? You want to watch that. Got my husband, that, you know, poor bugger. He's been gone thirteen years now.'

'I didn't know your husband was dead,' I said, trying to be considerate.

'He isn't, dear,' she laughed. 'He's gone to his sister's... He still drinks and smokes like a trooper, I don't know how she stands it,' she said, just as Roy Bennett came in.

'What are you doing here?' he asked. 'I thought you were in Sheffield Crown Court this morning doing a bail application.'

I felt beads of sweat on my forehead as I realised that I'd forgotten to put the application in my diary. I went to the filing cabinet, and of course, because it was urgent and I was late and desperate, couldn't find the file. Eventually it turned up, but not before I'd kicked the filing cabinet and tripped over the telephone wire.

I ran out to my car, which had been blocked in by a bread van, eventually escaped, and set off through town like the proverbial bat out of hell. Why is it that when you're in a rush you get stuck behind twelve learner drivers, five JCBs, and two broken-down milk floats? I'd dispensed my entire vocabulary of swear words by the time I found a parking place, and was still a quarter of a mile from the court. There was nothing else to do but to start running, and with about a minute to spare I reached Court Number Three, where an usher was waiting for me.

'Mr Smith,' I wheezed. 'Bail application, Morton, before Judge Walker, and have you got an iron lung?'

'Don't worry, Mr Smith, the judge won't be here for another thirty minutes. He's been delayed in traffic!' said the usher, as though I should have known. I slumped back on the seat outside the courtroom and wiped sweat from my brow with an ink-stained handkerchief.

Fifteen minutes later I was called into the judge's chambers to find him with not a bead of sweat on him. I, on the other hand, was saturated. The judge peered over his horn-rimmed glasses and said, 'Are you all right, Mr, er, Smith?'

'Perfectly, Your Honour,' I replied, wiping more sweat off and ink on.

'Well, I've looked at your bail application, Mr Smith,' said the judge. 'He's a wicked man, and wicked men must go to prison. I see no possibility of a non-custodial sentence, so he shall remain in custody on the grounds that he'll commit further offences if he's granted bail. Next case.'

I left the judge's chambers feeling that, while he had made the right decision, I wasn't too happy about the way he'd expressed it, but I suppose that was his prerogative. I ran down to the magistrates' court and, using the old pals act, managed to jump the queue, apart from one solicitor who wasn't prepared to be helpful.

A solicitor who had let me push in was sitting directly behind me, and when I eventually finished my case, I turned to him and said, 'Thanks a lot. When you come to Rotherham I'll do the same for you.' As I rushed out of the court I almost fell over the solicitor who had been less obliging, and said exactly the same to him.

I left the Sheffield court at 11.30, arriving back in Rotherham twenty minutes later, and ran into the courtroom, to be greeted by the emphysemic usher. 'Brilliant timing, Steve, there's just one case left and then it's you.'

'You mean there's no bollocking?'

'No bollocking at all, except perhaps from your clients,' he said.

'Oh, I can deal with that,' I said, and promptly called out the names of the people I was to represent. I recognised all but one, which was a file Roy had prepared and put in the diary for that morning. Looking for my client, I spotted an unusual looking person in a dark suit, with an Elvis Presley haircut.

'I'm Jane,' said Elvis in a deep, melodious voice. We shook hands and she crushed my knuckles, making me wince with pain.

We went to the 'rat hole' interview room, and I realised that this would need to be an adjournment, so we could obtain the evidence from the prosecution and consider how best to approach the case – the file had only been brought up to court for me that morning, and I hadn't had a chance to read it. It was an assault case, which had occurred in a night club a few days before, and the charge sheet referred to an S. Clarke.

'What's Miss Clarke's first name?' I asked.

'Simon,' she replied.

'Oh, right,' I said, adjusting my ideas. 'Well, the case is going to be adjourned today so we can see what the evidence is against you, but please tell me what happened.'

She explained that this youth had made some insulting remarks about her dress and hairstyle. 'He said, "He's a big bugger, and he's got his own tits as well." I hate sexist remarks like that, and I wasn't being humiliated by him or anybody, so I lamped him. I only hit him once, but it was a good 'un,' said my client, totally understating the position – I later found out that she had knocked out three of his front teeth and left his lip requiring four stitches.

When I got into court, I found the prosecutor also wanted an adjournment, because he was waiting for a further statement from a dentist to confirm how much treatment would be needed to replace the lost teeth. We came out into the corridor, and as I advised Jane about bail and the requirement to return to court on the date she'd been given, some idiot behind me passed a sexist remark. Jane's eyes narrowed and flashed in search of the culprit. 'Who said that?' she demanded angrily.

No one answered, and I ushered her away. Jane's temper

certainly had a hair trigger, so it was no surprise to me that she was well known to the courts, what with her physical strength.

That evening I met Jarvis and Co. at Sellors restaurant at Dronfield for our monthly soirée. Bob and Lynn, the owners, were extremely likable people, and as well as providing excellent food and service they had forgiving natures. I didn't intend to join in the more serious drinking due to an important football match the following day, but by the end of the evening I had somehow thoroughly enjoyed myself. The following morning I felt dreadful, and couldn't shake off the hangover, despite drinking many bottles of mineral water. At 5.30pm after a difficult day I set off to the match, changing in the car when I arrived at the ground.

We were playing the Probation Service team, intelligent and kindly people at work, but vicious fouling morons on the football field. In the first fifteen minutes, I had a least three clear chances to score, but fluffed each one.

Bader Lidster asked me what was wrong. 'I feel like death,' I told him.

'Is it a virus?' he asked sympathetically.

'Yes, I suppose you could say that, Bader. At any rate, the effects are similar.'

A little later in the game, we were awarded a free kick for a foul. 'You take this one, cocker,' said Bader.

I looked into the distance and saw the biggest goalkeeper in the world. Since my accuracy left a lot to be desired that day, I thought that if I aimed directly for him the ball might go near one of the posts. I took six or seven paces, ran up to the ball, and mis-kicked it. It spun off the side of my foot, arced round three players in the defensive wall, and shot into the top left-hand corner of the net like a guided missile. All the team congratulated me, and even our opponents gave a round of applause.

'Tha's taking all t'free kicks from now on,' said Bader. 'I nivver saw a ball struck like that before.'

I ran to the touchline and was violently sick, then returned and scored two more goals before coming off with ten minutes to go. After the match we went to the pub, where I ordered two bitter lemons and a sandwich. Bader came back with an egg, tomato and dripping sandwich, which was marvellous. There's something to be said for the hair of the dog, and two pints of Guinness later I felt on such good form I decided to go back to the office to collect some papers for a case I was dealing with the following day.

I had just picked up the papers and was about to leave when the telephone rang. You should never answer the telephone in an office after 5.30pm, because it always leads to trouble. Unfortunately, I broke the rule on this occasion, to be told that my client Jane had been involved in an altercation in a working men's club. Another girl had been seriously injured when a broken glass had slashed her neck, and was in a critical condition. I had no choice but to go the police station, see my client, and get an update on the girl's medical condition before considering the best course of action.

I arrived at the charge office to see a stern-faced custody sergeant Brown on the telephone.

'Yes sir, her solicitor's just arrived,' he said. 'No sir, she hasn't been told yet, I rather thought Mr Smith might...'

As Sergeant Brown listened to his instructions a shiver ran down my spine. 'Very good, sir,' he replied eventually. 'I'll ask him to wait for you to join us, sir.' He put the phone down and turned to me, but it wasn't a cheerful welcome.

'What's wrong, Dave?' I asked cautiously.

'Better wait for Chief Inspector Varey,' said the sergeant. 'I'm under orders.'

Chief Inspector Varey arrived, also grim-faced. Before he could speak I had realised what had happened.

'She's dead, isn't she, the girl in Jane Webb's case?'

The Chief Inspector gave Sergeant Brown an accusatory glare.

'Not a word, sir,' he defended himself. 'I think Mr Smith worked it out.'

'Well you're right,' said the Chief Inspector to me. 'About an hour ago: haemorrhage and shock. The main artery was severed, and the blood loss was too great. Her birthday's tomorrow; she would have been twenty-one. Happy birthday, eh?'

I sat in the chair usually occupied by defendants having their photo taken for CID records. 'I take it she doesn't know?' I queried, nodding towards the female cells.

'No, she doesn't,' said Chief Inspector Varey. 'I thought you might want to tell her, and then I'm afraid we've got to do an interview. Of course, if you prefer me to…?'

His words tailed off reluctantly.

'No, it's OK, I'll tell her. Which cell is she in?'

I was directed to the cell, where I found Jane sitting cross-legged, forlorn and lonely. Her eyes lit up when she saw me, but unfortunately, I couldn't return her smile, and she realised that I was not the bearer of good news. We looked at each other in a silence that seemed interminable, until Jane spoke.

'You've got something to tell me, haven't you?'

I looked away, and she knew before I could open my mouth. She burst into tears, and I simply sat beside her as her body shook with sobs. She was distraught, and there was nothing I could say to help her.

After some time she quietened, and I handed her a packet of cigarettes. She smoked furiously, lighting one cigarette after the other, until the cell was thick with smoke. I rang the bell to get her a drink, and the jailer brought in a glass of weak orange squash. I persuaded him to let us go into the exercise area, and with the fresh air and rehydration Jane began to regain her composure.

I'd just asked her what had happened when there was a terrific clap of thunder, and the heavens opened. I dashed for the doorway, but Jane remained motionless, leaning against the wall and staring down at the ground. Rainwater mixed with fresh tears as she began to shake again, clearly just realising the enormity of what had happened. After a few minutes a policewoman took her gently by the arm and escorted her into the charge office. With her shoulders bowed and her hair hanging wet and limp, Jane had shrunk into just a frightened young woman. I suggested they leave her alone for a little, and Sergeant Brown rang her parents to ask them to bring her a change of clothes.

Mr and Mrs Webb were in their late fifties or early sixties, and the first thing that struck me about them was that they didn't look like a couple. He was trim-waisted and clean-shaven, smartly dressed in cavalry twill trousers and a sports jacket with sleeves that had been intended for someone with longer arms, and had obviously taken Henry Cooper's advice to 'splash on the Brut'. Mrs Webb, on the other hand, had not worn well. Her eyes were care-worn, and alongside her husband she looked an insignificant fig-ure, in dowdy clothes covered by a worn-out long brown mac. She carried a bulging shopping bag, and trembled as I explained what had happened.

Mr Webb remained silent as I imparted my grim tidings, though his lips quivered, as if tears were near. His wife became dis-traught and he tried to console her, but it was a task he wasn't comfortable with. To give them some privacy I volunteered to take Jane's clothes into the cell area, where she had had a shower and a cup of tea. As I came back to the charge office counter, the detec-tive inspector in charge of the inquiry, who was inappropriately named Meek, presented himself, and informed me he was ready to start the interview.

I returned to Jane's cell to see if she was also ready. She was clean and tidy, and her hair was combed backwards: strands of it had begun to stick out as they dried.

'I didn't mean to kill her, Mr Smith,' said Jane. 'I didn't realise I had a glass in my hand. It was just an instant reaction. I never meant this to happen.'

I believed her, but Jane's problem was to convince the detective inspector who, like many of his rank, had been there before and seen it all.

I left the cell and told him Jane was ready for the interview, but first I asked his view as to what had happened.

'You can't tell me she didn't intend to cause grievous bodily harm. She might not have intended to kill, but I only have to prove that she intended GBH to establish murder.'

'I don't think she did,' I replied. 'She says she didn't realise she had the glass in her hand. I think she'd been grossly affected by drink and her immediate reaction was to strike out. I haven't seen any evidence that she broke the glass before using it, which tends to support her story, doesn't it?'

'We'll see,' said the detective inspector, and strode into the interview room, where Jane was already waiting. His attitude changed the moment he entered. He smiled at Jane and asked if she would like a drink. This was all part and parcel of his act, of course, lulling his subject into a false sense of security before delivering the killer punch.

'Hello Jane,' he began. 'I'm Detective Inspector Meek, and I have to interview you about this case. I'll try to be brief, and if you feel up to it I'd like to start now.'

Before she could answer, he had started to write out the caution on the notes he would take contemporaneously, working on automatic pilot. Any second now, I thought, he'll smile and say, 'Now then, Jane, tell us what happened,' and lo and behold, he did.

Jane related her story as best she could, but parts of the tale were confused and unclear. Her voice wavered, interrupted at times by gasps as she tried to keep her composure, and tears kept welling up in her eyes. She said she had drunk maybe twelve pints of lager and, as she put it, the odd brandy and Babycham – a lethal mixture, even without her volatile temper. She had been dancing when the complainant, whose tongue had been loosened by drink, made certain offensive comments to her friends. Jane couldn't hear the exact words, but the girl's gesticulations were enough for her to recognise the general drift.

As the evening progressed, Jane was subjected to more and more humiliation. At first she ignored it, and even went to the other side of the dance floor, but the girl and her party followed her and the taunting persisted. On one occasion, she warned the girl that if she didn't stop pestering her she would 'bottle' her. This, I knew, would be one of the major points supporting the prosecution's claim that the assault was premeditated.

Jane then began taking her drinks onto the dance floor, which wasn't allowed, but the club was busy and the bouncers hadn't noticed. At approximately 1.45am, when the delirium on the dance floor was at its height, the victim danced behind Jane simulating thrusting motions with her hips. Unfortunately Jane saw, and instantly swung her fist towards the girl's face. Her glass hit the girl's neck, smashing on impact (the palm of Jane's hand was also cut quite badly).

It was some seconds before anyone moved, but eventually the door staff were alerted, the crowd moved back, and the police and an ambulance were called. Jane, who had made no attempt to leave the scene, was led away by the police.

Detective Inspector Meek listened intently, scribbling furiously to keep up with Jane's account, but the corner of his mouth twitched, signalling his reluctance to accept what she was saying.

'Did you intend to kill her?' he asked with the finesse of a steam hammer.

'No,' replied Jane, equally forcefully.

He persisted with this line of questioning for over an hour, but Jane stuck to her story, that she had no intention of either killing the girl or indeed causing grievous bodily harm.

'You must have known you were holding a glass,' persisted the inspector. 'If you hadn't known, you'd have dropped it. And isn't it right, Jane, that if you hit someone with a glass you can expect them to be badly injured? Why don't you admit it? Think of that poor girl's parents. She was an only child. Can you imagine how they feel?'

The old heart-strings routine came at the end of a long day and very stressful interview, and I was considering whether it was fair, when Jane answered, 'Yes, I suppose so.'

I was alarmed, because Meek was talking her into admitting that she expected to cause grievous bodily harm, which would make his case. But as I understood her, Jane was saying that she understood how the parents must feel, so I interrupted and asked for the point to be clarified. This ruffled Meek's feathers, and he went back to the point about the glass.

'You were having a drink, weren't you?' he continued. 'Well, what were you drinking it out of?'

'I suppose a glass,' said Jane.

'Well, where was the glass?' said Meek.

'I suppose it was in my hand,' she said.

'So you did realise you were holding it, then?' he persisted. Before I could interrupt again, Jane replied, 'No, I didn't. I'm just agreeing that if I had a glass and was drinking from it, it would be in my hand.'

Meek sensed victory. 'Well then, so you accept that you knew you had a glass in your hand at the time of the blow?'

'I don't know. I don't know what's going on,' said Jane, and burst into tears. I used the break in the proceedings to remind Meek of her earlier comments about the glass, and asked Jane to clarify the position once again, which she did satisfactorily.

Meek took another tack. 'Do you remember, when the girl was dancing, if she was in a group?'

'No,' said Jane thoughtfully. 'It happened so quickly I didn't notice who she was with.'

'Well, we have a witness who says she saw you move some five or six steps towards the girl before the assault took place. What do you say to that?'

'I can't remember that,' said Jane. 'All I remember is turning round and seeing her doing or saying something, and just hitting out.'

Meek continued almost as if she hadn't answered, reading from the witness statement. ' "The girl was looking at Shirley so aggressively I was afraid there'd be trouble. I saw there was a glass in her hand, but I can't recall whether it had anything in it. She then pushed the glass into Shirley's face. Shirley tried to move out of the way, but the glass hit her neck so hard that it smashed. My opinion was that this had been done intentionally." '

I was unhappy about her 'opinion', but Jane countered quite well. 'She's her best friend; she's bound to stick up for her. She'll be angry with me because of what happened, and trying to get me into trouble.'

Meek recapped the facts once again before concluding, 'I put it to you that if you didn't intend to murder Shirley, you did intend to do her grievous bodily harm.'

'Neither,' said Jane defiantly.

'Well, that's for the jury to decide,' said Meek, and concluded the interview. Old habits die hard with seasoned CID officers, and he then started chatting to Jane, asking further questions. I immediately advised her not to answer, as the conversation wasn't being recorded. Meek looked at me, shook his head, and said, 'Really, Mr Smith!' as though I should have been ashamed of interfering. I've always been disappointed in police officers who seem unable to accept that we have a job to do, just like them.

He then announced that he would be charging Jane with murder.

'Murder?' she said slowly.

'Yes, murder, Miss Webb. I believe that you intended to kill the girl, and what's more, I intend to prove it.' With that, Meek left the room, and walked down the corridor whistling 'Happy Birthday to you'.

I returned to Mr and Mrs Webb to explain what was happening, and told them that Jane would be remanded in custody overnight, but they might be able to see her after she was charged. Sure enough, once the formalities were complete the Webbs were asked to wait in an interview room and Jane was brought in to them. The unacceptability of untimely death had affected us all, but Jane's father in particular. He walked, head bowed, from the interview room to the foyer and then out into the street, a broken man being led by his wife.

I bumped into Meek as I left.

'Juries don't like dykes,' he said. 'The odds are against her.' Then he had an afterthought. 'She'll get on well in a woman's prison, they'll like her!' Detective Inspector Meek whistled 'Strangers in the Night' as he set off for the tearoom.

Next morning the court refused Jane's bail application, not only because she was facing a very serious charge, but because she had committed the alleged offence while on bail for the other matter. She was taken to HM Prison Risley, near Warrington, which is an awful two-hour drive, weaving in and out of lines of lorries and various road works on the M62. In all the years I've travelled on the motorway, I cannot recall one trip free of road works.

The prison houses remands, people in custody pending trial or sentence, and is divided into two sections for male and female prisoners. The walk from reception to the prison itself is known as the 'Valley of a Thousand Cuts', as it is overlooked by the women's cells. Anyone walking through is subjected to a torrent of shouts and taunts, which can either inflate your ego or destroy it absolutely. Cries of 'Get 'em off' and 'Show us your arse' are commonplace, and many of the requests and suggestions are interesting, but physically impossible.

Visits take place in a large room like a meeting hall, where small tables and tubular chairs are laid out in regimental rows. Starting time was 9.15am and chuck-out time 11.30am. It seemed a long way to travel for only a two-hour visit, and inevitably I had to make the journey several times.

The female warders were an interesting group, some of whom would have done well against the American heavyweight boxing champion of the day, Larry Holmes. One in particular, who used to greet me at the gates and take me to the special visits centre, bore a marked resemblance to the wrestler Mick McManus, but for the moustache.

As was allowed then, I always brought cigarettes, which were valuable items on the black market – drugs hadn't yet become as freely available as they would in later years. Jane presented a very different picture in the prison setting. She had lost a great deal of weight, her face was putty-coloured, and to her embarrassment she was plagued with cold sores. We discussed the case over and over again in the weeks leading up to the trial, and each interview ended in the same way, with Jane asking me for a prediction as to result. Each time my reply had to be the same: 'I just don't know.'

EIGHTEEN

JANE'S TRIAL AND THE CASE OF THE FALSE LEG

The first day of Jane's case eventually came. Trials can be won or lost at this stage, because if the jury gets a bad impression of the defendant they're against him or her from the start. I had advised Jane to sit quietly with her eyes down, and not to interrupt the questions in any way, no matter how annoyed some of them might make her.

The first witness was the deceased girl's best friend. She was smartly dressed, presented a good impression, and gave a good account of herself, but then Peter Baker, our defence counsel, cross-examined her and decided to put in her record, meaning that he told the jury about her criminal convictions. This worked, and her evidence was discredited. I believe the jury shared my view, that she had stretched the truth for reasons of revenge.

On the second day of the trial, I went to visit Jane in the cells, but she wasn't there. The staff told me she had cut her wrists the night before, so the case had been adjourned for forty-eight hours to enable her to recover and return to court. I had cases in Rotherham and Barnsley that day, but had called on colleagues to take them for me, so I was looking forward to some 'free' time in the office to deal with paperwork when the charge office at Rotherham police station contacted me.

'Hello, Mr Smith,' said Sergeant Brown. 'I thought you were in a murder trial in Sheffield?'

'I was,' I said, 'but it's a long story. What can I do for you?'

'Well, we have two young men here requiring your services. They've been arrested on suspicion of theft of…' His words tailed off to silence.

'Hello, hello Dave, are you there?' I shouted.

'Yes,' said Sergeant Brown contemplatively. 'Sorry about that, I was just reading the reasons for the arrest, which can't be right. Just hold on a minute.'

I heard him speak to a colleague. 'This can't be right, Fred, can it? Theft of a leg.'

I also heard Fred reply, 'Yes, Sarge, it's true as I am standing here, but I think you should insert the word "aluminium" before leg.'

'What the bloody hell's gone off?' said the sergeant, then the conversation stopped when the two officers moved away from the phone.

Dave eventually returned to the phone and told me he'd explain everything when I got there. I checked my watch and decided to go straight away, in the hope of finishing in time to get back for lunch at the Keys. As I left reception, I noticed a man I didn't know making an appointment to see me: he was on crutches, and I distinctly heard the words 'theft' and 'compensation' spoken in a strong eastern European accent. But I didn't have time to wait, so I scooted out of the office and was down at the police station within five minutes.

Owen and Desmond Gillis were two local ne'er-do-wells who would do anything for a laugh. The day before they had excelled themselves, when they embarked on a scheme suggested for a bet. Anatole Stosik was a Polish war veteran who had settled in England after the war, having lost his leg in action. Recently the British Legion had got him a new aluminium leg to replace his wooden one, a splendid piece of modern technology noticeable only by a slight limp, heavier during cold weather. Mr Stosik wore specially made trousers with press studs down the side of the left leg for ease of release. He was famous with the local children because when he was drunk – which was quite often, especially on a Friday after he'd collected his pension – he would remove the leg and do Long John Silver impressions, to their great amusement. He would then sleep it off in the local park.

The Gillis brothers had been in the British Legion that day and seen Mr Stosik drink himself into his usual state. I don't know who suggested it, but the regulars agreed that if they could steal Mr Stosik's leg and bring it back to the bar, they'd all chip in and give them £10 each.

So Owen and Desmond followed Mr Stosik and waited until he lapsed into sleep on a park bench. Carefully, so as not to wake him, they undid the studs along his left trouser leg, unstrapped the aluminium limb, and ran off gleefully with their prize. They received their reward, but after three renditions of 'I'm Jake the Peg' the crowd got bored, and the landlord told the brothers he didn't want stolen property on his premises, so they should find Mr Stosik and give him his leg back.

Meanwhile, back at the park, Mr Stosik was coming round from his siesta, the sleep having sobered him up somewhat. But it wasn't until he actually stood up that he realised he was legless, and for once it had nothing to do with his alcohol intake. He immediately began hopping to the nearest police station, collecting an entourage of children who hopped after him.

The Gillis brothers arrived back at the park hoping to be able to replace the leg before Mr Stosik woke up. When they saw he had gone, whatever good intentions they might have had disappeared, and they took the leg to the local scrap dealer, who weighed it and gave them twenty pence to go away.

The police gave Mr Stosik a pair of crutches and his bus fare, and had no trouble in nailing the culprits, because the victim of an earlier prank by the Gillis brothers had been at the Legion when they had come in holding the leg aloft. He informed the police, and within the hour they had been arrested. After much hilarity during the interviews, admissions were made, charges laid, and bail granted. Fortunately, the scrap dealer hadn't yet done anything with the leg, and the police were able to return it to its grateful owner.

(When the case came to court a week later, the Gillis brothers were fined and ordered to pay compensation to Mr Stosik, who became something of a local celebrity when the *Rotherham Advertiser* reported the case and stressed his war record. In fact, Anatoli Stosik was a 'leg-end' in his own lifetime – sorry!)

My visit to the police station provided some light relief, but put me behind schedule. I was cursing the fact when I arrived back at the office to find Tracy had just taken an unwelcome phone call.

'Crown Court on line one,' she said.

'Oh, flipping heck,' I replied, and took it. 'Hello, General Dogsbody here. How can I inconvenience myself to suit your convenience?'

'Oh hello, this is the Crown Court. Your case of Jane Webb will continue at 2.15pm.'

It was 1.30pm, and the journey to Sheffield was at least thirty minutes. 'Oh brilliant,' I said. 'Thanks for all the notice, and how do you think I'm going to get there on time? A helicopter, perhaps?'

'That's your problem,' came the reply. 'I've given you the message and that's it.' Before I could give forth a mixed range of expletives, the caller rang off.

'Bastards!' I announced under my breath, and set off for Sheffield.

I arrived with five minutes to spare, so I visited Jane in the holding cell beneath the court. She was a forlorn figure, dressed in a plain blue suit, her hair left untidy, her face pale and drawn, and fresh bandages, stained with blood from the two self-inflicted wounds around her wrists.

'Why, Jane?' I asked as gently as possible.

'It's all right for you. You don't know what I'm going through. I can't face going to prison for life, I just can't,' she said tearfully.

'But you don't know the result yet. You have a real chance of getting manslaughter,' I replied forcefully.

'You don't understand,' said Jane. 'I killed someone... She's dead, and it's my fault, it's my conscience. I can't live with that. I'm guilty, I know it now. I want to plead guilty.'

'You can't do that,' I replied, almost indignantly. 'We're halfway through the trial. You can't just throw it in now. For God's sake, pull yourself together.'

'For God's sake, you say. And what'll God think of me? Please, leave me alone.'

I did my best to comfort her, and for a moment thought I'd succeeded, but we were interrupted by a jailer who told us the court was waiting. I returned to the courtroom and listened to the remaining witnesses. Matters were beginning to go our way, and at the end of the prosecution case the counsel for the prosecution took ours to one side. I asked what was going on, and Peter Baker told me they were considering whether to accept manslaughter, but advised me not to say anything to Jane in case it turned out to be a false hope. However, I thought it might just keep her spirits up for the rest of the trial and so, not for the first time, followed my instinct against advice.

Down in her cell, Jane was sitting alone staring into space. She was holding a Bible, a page turned over at the corner as a marker. There was no recognition in her face, and she didn't acknowledge me in any way.

'Jane, I've got some news for you. The prosecution's... Jane, are you listening to me?' I asked.

Just then, the jailer entered. 'Your parents are here, Jane. You can have a visit if you want, but you only have two minutes. The bus is here to take you back, and the driver has another pick-up.'

Jane nodded acceptance, and turned and smiled at me. She held out her hand and I shook it gently. It seemed that she had found an inner peace, but I was troubled without knowing why.

Her parents appeared at the glass partition. None of them spoke. Mr Webb looked tired and ill, and Mrs Webb was in tears.

Jane finally said, 'It's all right, Mum. I'm all right now. Everything's all right, I promise; you don't need to worry any more. I'll be fine where I'm going.'

She pressed her palm against the glass, and her parents did the same. The moment was intensely moving, and it seemed wrong to interrupt it. That was left to the jailer, who'd been in the job too long to be moved.

'But Jane, I must tell you what's happening!' I called after them as he led her away. 'Just a moment!'

'Tomorrow,' replied the jailer. 'It'll wait.'

'Insolent bastard,' I said under my breath as I listened to the sound of the clinking keys on his massive key ring.

'What's wrong with Jane?' asked her mother. 'I've never seen her like that before. How strange she was!'

'Don't worry,' I said. 'I'll see her first thing in the morning. I'm sure she'll be OK.'

The following morning I arrived at court to be told formally that the prosecution were prepared, having considered the evidence given in the trial, to accept a guilty plea to a charge of manslaughter, providing the judge agreed. I set off for the cells as quickly as I could, but the bus hadn't yet arrived. I sat on the wooden bench and perused the graffiti-laden walls. The ceilings were brown from years of nicotine staining, and the whole area reeked of stale tobacco and body odour, warring with the smell of frying bacon drifting from the jailers' rest room. Noticing a small Bible on the seat in the corner, I picked it up and saw the name written on the inside cover. It read:

JANE WEBB
THRYBERGH COMPREHENSIVE 1975

The corner of one page was folded over. The chapter was headed Exodus 22, and almost as if I knew where to look, I read verse 24: 'Eye for eye, tooth for tooth, hand for hand and foot for foot.'

Before I could read any further, a vast, white-shirted female prison officer walked into the doorway, blocking out the light. 'Are you Mr Smith, Jane Webb's solicitor?' she asked quietly.

'Yes. What can I do for you?' I replied.

'I'm afraid I have bad news for you,' she said, without altering the inflection in her voice.

'It's Jane, isn't it?' I said intuitively.

'Yes. The court has already been informed. She's dead,' she said, resisting the urge to tell me gently. 'She used her pillowcase – tore it up and made a rope. We found her this morning. She was in a cell on her own, rule 43 protection, you know. The doctor said she'd been dead for hours. There was no note or anything.'

'No,' I said, in a state of shock but nevertheless realising what last night's farewell had meant. 'There wouldn't be.' I turned to leave, but the officer's words stopped me.

'Has she anyone here… family or anything?'

'Er, yes,' I replied. 'Her parents. I'm sorry, I'm a little shocked.'

'Well she was just a client, wasn't she? There's plenty of others, and it's one less for the taxpayer to pay for…' She wandered off without waiting for my reply – which was just as well, as I couldn't think of one, certainly not without swearing.

Jane's parents were in the foyer. They both stood up when I walked in, Mr Webb holding his cap and Mrs Webb her handbag, but Detective Inspector Meek got to me first.

'Have you heard?' he said gravely.

'Yes – just.'

'Hanging, wasn't it? What about them?' he asked, referring to Jane's parents. 'They don't know yet. Look, I'll tell them,' he offered.

I took his arm. 'No, I'll see them. I'd rather it came from me.' I turned away and walked over to Mr and Mrs Webb.

'Is everything OK, Mr Smith?' asked Jane's father.

I didn't answer, but led them to an interview room, changed the marker on the door from vacant to engaged, and closed it. This was going to take some time.

NINETEEN

AS FAR AS I'M CONCERNED, I'M THE EARL OF SCARBOROUGH

Working in the legal profession you certainly see life – and indeed, all too frequently, death. The saying 'but for fools and rogues' sits well with the profession, which certainly has a constant queue of rogues waiting to be dealt with. But we mustn't forget the fools, either.

Geoffrey Samuel Plowright was one such. Many suggested that he wasn't so much a fool as stark raving mad, so far gone even the mental hospitals wouldn't take him. It wasn't possible to get two consultant psychiatrists to agree about him, which was a problem, because two such opinions are required before a hospital order can be made.

Geoffrey didn't accept that he was mad, and the very suggestion would send him into a frenzy that could be calmed only by an injection or a big mallet. His condition worsened over the years I knew him, aggravated by tremendous mood swings and fits of depression. He could be perfectly reasonable, if eccentric, but at other times he could be utterly irrational. He was also six foot six inches tall, weighed eighteen stone, with a shiny bald head and dark piercing eyes – rather like Rasputin without the hair.

One afternoon, when I was in the midst of a massive appointment list, Geoffrey appeared at reception and frightened poor Tracy by letting his eyes roll up into his head and pretending to be a Dalek.

'Is…he…in…please… I …need…help…they…tried to poison me…at the Cross Keys.'

'Oh, you've had the steak and kidney pie, then?' said Tracy, well used to weirdoes.

I led him into my office and sat him down.

'Paraquat,' said Geoffrey forcefully. 'In the beer – well, in my beer at least, and they did it.'

'They?' I asked.

'Yes,' said Geoffrey, banging his hand on the desk. 'Yes, but we'll get them, Montmorency. I want to sue them.'

I didn't pursue the 'Montmorency' bit. 'Why would anyone want to poison you, Geoffrey?' I asked, trying to play the close friendship card.

'Because I'm really the Earl of Scarborough!'

This surprised me so much the only thing I could think of to say was that I'd never met a real Earl before.

'I should be referred to as my liege,' said Geoffrey.

'Very well, my liege,' I said, trying to humour him. 'Would you like a Woodbine?'

'Earls don't smoke!' was the reply. 'I want you to act quickly. Report to me by the end of the week,' and with that he took his leave, shouting 'Paraquat' as he left.

'That was the Earl of Scarborough. They're poisoning him,' I announced to my old friend Jack, who was my next appointment.

'Good idea. He's a zit,' said Jack.

'A what?' I asked.

'A zit,' said Jack. 'Tha knows what that is, dun't tha?'

'Of course,' I replied, none the wiser. 'Now what's to do, Jack?'

'Nowt for me,' said Jack. 'It's our 'orace, tha sees. He's gone and got nicked for pinching, but it weren't 'im. They've set 'im up, tha knows, bastard coppers.'

'What's he supposed to have done?'

'Nicked all them johnnies from that lorry at Boots,' said Jack cryptically. I had long since realised that I needed a can opener to get information out of Jack. He would give me minor snippets of a story, leaving me to uncover the rest by a process of elimination.

'What lorry?' I asked.

'That lorry wi' deliveries on,' said Jack, as if I should know the movements of every haulage truck in Rotherham.

'OK, I think I've got it,' I said. 'There's a delivery lorry taking goods to Boots, yes? And someone entered the lorry and stole some of its contents?'

'Not some,' said Jack, as if he were privy to a great secret. 'All of it! Full bag o' mashings, the lot, maximum, all on't, everything, full Monty… Tha knows.'

'Anything else?' I asked sarcastically.

'Argh,' said Jack, nodding in approval. 'Container.'

'You mean they stole the container as well?'

'Argh,' said Jack. 'And t'lorry that pulled it. Nowt left.'

'And your Horace is thought to be responsible?'

'Argh, but it weren't him,' he said knowingly.

'I'll have to see your Horace before he's interviewed.'

'Argh,' said Jack. ''E'll come in and see thee whenever tha wants him. Soon, though, 'cos coppers want 'im tomorrow neet.'

'OK Jack, I'll see him tomorrow at 5pm, if that's OK. What did you say the lorry's load was?'

'Johnnies,' said Jack.

'Johnnie's what?' I asked in confusion.

'Tha knows, johnnies,' said Jack, perplexed at my inability to comprehend the obvious. 'Johnnies…rubbers…sheaths…covers…skins…Catholic hats…Ee, by 'eck, CONDOMS! Fourteen thousand boxes, apparently,' he added with verve.

I had visions of the Rotherham branch of Boots taking delivery of that amount of rubber goods, and imagined we must be the condom centre of South Yorkshire, but my ideas were altered by Jack's explanation.

'They weren't all for Rotherham, tha knows, there was more than wun shop to deliver to.'

'I wonder if the thief knew what the lorry was carrying?' I asked Jack.

'He certainly did when 'e gorrit 'ome,' said Jack.

'They'd last quite a bit,' I suggested, and we both laughed. But it occurred to me that Jack's knowledge of the shipment was suspicious, to say the least. I remembered the last time Jack had acquired goods from a lorry – the cigars – and my imagination ran wild, with visions of court corridors and tearooms full of men wearing stolen condoms.

'Bloody hell,' I said. 'Who'd want to steal that lot?'

'I don't think they knew what were in t'lorry. They'd be after scent and electrical stuff, tha knows. There's not much call for condoms around our end,' said Jack, and I became certain that he had more than a supporting role in the venture.

'Why did the police pick on your Horace?' I asked.

'They foun' 'em in his loft,' said Jack thoughtfully. 'All on 'em except wun box. But just cos 'e got them in 'is loft dun't mean he nicked 'em.'

'No, but it certainly puts him firmly in the frame. Well, get Horace to come in and see me tomorrow and we'll see what we can do.'

I showed Jack out, and returned to my room in time to answer a telephone call from the local police station.

'Good afternoon, Mr Smith, this is Sergeant Suter. I have a client of yours locked up, and demanding to see you before he's interviewed. If you could call down to see him it would help us, because he won't give us his real name. He says he's Geoffrey, the Earl of Scarborough.'

'Is he a big, bald-headed bugger with wild eyes?' I asked.

'Yes, that's the one,' said the sergeant. 'He came into our reception demanding that we arrest everybody in the Cross Keys for poisoning him. He was asked to leave, but he refused, so we had to arrest him for breaching the peace. He was threatening to go back to the Cross Keys and poison them in return. We can't let him out in this state. We're thinking about getting a psychiatrist to come and see if he's suitable for a section.'

'Suitable for a section' means that a consultant psychiatrist believes a mentally ill person is unfit to remain at liberty. Usually, they are taken to the local hospital and placed in the psychiatric wing, where they are drugged and monitored over a period of twenty-eight days.

'Don't tell him you're bringing in a psychiatrist just yet,' I warned the sergeant. 'Let me put that to him when I get there.'

At the station, the careworn sergeant called a young constable to go to Lord Scarborough's cell and bring him to be interviewed.

'Would you be kind enough, officer, to fetch My Lord the Earl of Scarborough so that his solicitor and confidant Mr Smith can have the opportunity of discussing his present legal problem?'

'Which cell is he in, Sarge?' asked the fresh-faced policeman, who appeared to have just started shaving.

The sergeant turned to his small blackboard showing the cell occupancy, which showed the word 'loony' alongside cell four. The recipient of this rather discourteous title was brought out, and the sergeant bowed low before he spoke.

'My Lord, Mr Smith has arrived to see you. Mr Smith, I have pleasure in introducing to you My Lord the Earl of Scarborough.'

Geoffrey thanked the sergeant graciously before turning to me. 'After you, Smith, I wish to speak with you in private.'

I made my way to a small interview room near the charge office. I'd planned to break it gently to Geoffrey that a psychiatrist had been requested, but I lost my bottle, and tried to approach the issue from a different standpoint.

'How are you feeling, My Lord? You don't look very well to me. In fact, you look really under the weather.'

'Do I really?' said the Earl. 'Now you come to mention it, I don't feel too well.'

'A man of your standing should have a medical check, whether the police like it or not,' I said, feigning concern for his welfare. 'I don't care whether the police will be inconvenienced or not; I'll *demand* that you be seen by a doctor.'

'Quite right,' said the Earl. 'Yes, we'll demand it. I'll speak to the sergeant myself.' He walked out of the interview room and approached the sergeant, who looked at him with dismay. 'I demand to see a doctor!'

'We're not bothered what sort of doctor it is, providing it's not a vet, but we wish one to be called straight away,' I chipped in.

The sergeant entered into the spirit of the ruse. 'Does that mean any doctor at all, Mr Smith?'

'Any at all,' I confirmed, 'rather than keep My Lord waiting.'

'Certainly,' said the sergeant. 'I'll deal with it straight away.'

'Quite right,' said the Earl, and walked back to the interview room. I winked at the sergeant, and followed Geoffrey to read the jokes in three-year-old *Readers' Digest* magazines while we waited.

The hospital had an on-call psychiatrist in the area, and within thirty minutes he was at the police station interviewing Geoffrey. Fifteen minutes later, the sergeant and I were disappointed in his report.

'There's nothing wrong with him,' he said. 'It's true he's slightly eccentric, but I don't think there's an ounce of aggression in him.' This was said straight-faced against a backing track of shouting and the smashing of such furniture as was in the cell.

I made my apologies and left, only to be contacted about an hour later and told that the gentle giant had attacked three police officers and a police dog. Geoffrey was charged with assaulting all three officers, and a curious charge of criminal damage, which read: 'That you caused criminal damage in that you did bite one police dog called Sherlock, causing damage to the said dog.' He was to be detained until the following day, when I would have to make a bail application before the local magistrates.

The courts always tried to deal with prisoners first, and that day was no exception. Before Geoffrey was called, I explained my difficulty with him to Keith Copley, the clerk of the court, and also that he wouldn't answer to his real name. I pointed out that if the court persisted in calling him Geoffrey Plowright he would cause trouble in the dock, and we would get nowhere. Keith entered into the spirit of things, and dealt with His Lordship masterfully.

'Are you Geoffrey Samuel Plowright...' Keith paused as if embarrassed before continuing '...otherwise known as the Earl of Scarborough?'

'I'm Lord Scarborough, what of it?' said Geoffrey defiantly.

Keith read out the charges. 'It is said that you, Geoffrey, Earl of Scarborough, did on the fourth day of December assault PC Calladine in the execution of his duty, contrary to section 51 of the Police Act 1954. Are you guilty or not guilty?'

'How dare you?' shouted the Earl.

I rose to my feet. 'May it please Your Worships, this is my application for an adjournment. I am seeking an extension of legal aid to facilitate the preparation of a report as to fitness to plead,' I said, wording it carefully to avoid upsetting the Earl. Fortunately the chairman took the point, and the adjournment was granted.

'Take him down,' said the chairman, and Geoffrey was whisked away by three of the largest constables in South Yorkshire Police.

Just then, the emphysemic usher passed me a note: 'New client in the cells, Horace Heptonstall, charged with burglary.' Almost at the same time, Jack appeared at the courtroom door, gesticulating vigorously.

'What happened last night?' I asked him. 'I was there, but no Horace.'

'Sorry about that, Steve,' said Jack. 'He buggered off, no one knew where. Then this morning a little bird told me he was locked up, so I came 'ere.'

'Why didn't he contact me?' I said, surprised.

'Tha knows our 'Orace, 'e wouldn't want to bother thee at neet.'

One of the nicest qualities of this family, despite their peculiarities, was also one of the rarest among a solicitor's clients – they didn't want to be a nuisance outside business hours. Brilliant!

Armed with my notebook, legal aid forms, and a bread-and-dripping sandwich courtesy of Jack, I went to see Horace, who was a nice lad, but not the brightest even by Heptonstall standards. He was sitting in cell number one, the one with the broken toilet, and enough graffiti to keep you reading for a full day.

'Now then, Horace!' I greeted him.

'Eh oop,' said Horace. 'Can tha get me bail? Only I've 'ad nowt to eat and I think I've got summat.' This meant that his incarceration had brought about a condition known colloquially as the shits.

'I've got my work cut out, Horace,' I said, handing him the sandwich, 'but with a bit of luck we should get you conditional bail.'

'Fookin' 'ell,' protested Horace, 'it were only a few fookin' johnnies.'

'No,' I replied, 'it was a trailer-load, and you've been found with them. Not to put too fine a point on it, you have to explain why you have stolen material in your possession so soon after the burglary.'

'Tha wha'?' said Horace.

'Well,' I translated, 'You had the bent gear right after the burglary, which suggests you had something to do with the burglary itself.'

'Bollocks,' said Horace. 'It means fook all. Any road, I dun't use 'em.' I believed him, as he was the father of five children, one born every year since his marriage. 'I'll 'ave 'andling,' he offered.

'Quite so,' I replied. 'I don't think you've much alternative. But what on earth did you get involved for?'

'I thought it were electrical gear, like,' said Horace evasively, and shut up shop. I took his instructions as quickly as possible, and returned to Court Number One, where Keith Copley was waiting for me with the prosecutor, Fred Jukes. I asked Fred if he was opposing bail, and sure enough he was.

'Why?' I asked. 'He's no current convictions, he's not on bail, and his father will drive me mad if he's not let out.'

'The police want a local remand,' said Fred. 'They think he's been bang at it and want to interview him further. They suspect he's committed other offences.'

'Bloody marvellous,' I said. 'What do I tell his father?'

'That his son's being locked up,' said Fred.

'You tell him,' I replied, and Fred coughed. He was an experienced prosecutor, and he certainly didn't fancy a new nose job.

Magistrates are reluctant to grant bail in such circumstances for fear they might be letting a guilty man get away with it, and Horace was remanded to the local cells for three days, a disappointment for him and his father and also for me. But in the event the police and magistrates were right, for during the remand Horace admitted twelve other offences of burglary, involving thousands of pounds' worth of property.

On his return to the court, Fred was again the prosecutor. 'We don't object to conditional bail,' he told me, 'providing he agrees a condition of residence, curfew between 8pm and 8am, reports to the police station each day at 6pm, and stops burgling local shops. But if he offends on bail, he's for it!'

I couldn't argue with that, so didn't. Horace was bailed, Jack was happy, and all was well for the time being.

I spoke to Jack outside the court. 'He seems to have admitted lots of offences,' I ventured.

'Argh,' said Jack. 'But he's only covering up for some bugger else.'

'And who might that be, Jack?' I asked.

Jack shrugged in acknowledgement that he knew exactly who else was involved, but I didn't press the point. We shook hands, and Jack left, with Albert bringing up the rear. The Heptonstall family loyalty was strong, even to the point of taking the blame for another relative's wrongdoings. Most criminals spend their time blaming their faults on others, but Jack's family were a one-off.

On Sunday afternoon I answered a telephone call that ruined my day. I had two clients in custody, the Earl of Scarborough and McIver, aka Spider. Geoffrey had fallen out with his next-door neighbour and hit him repeatedly around the head with a frying pan, while Spider had been caught with £1,000 worth of heroin. The two cases couldn't have been more diverse.

At the police station, I saw two other men, injured and battle-worn; they'd been fighting outside a town-centre pub, and seemed hell bent on doing it again in the charge office. A woman being booked in on prostitution allegations winked at me and mouthed 'I love you.' I winked back and said, 'I know.' And then there was the Earl...

When the 'customers' had been shown to their 'rooms', the custody sergeant greeted me with his usual charm. 'Two beauties for you today, Mr Smith.'

'Looks like it,' I replied. 'Who's Mr Plowright today – the Earl of Scarborough, Napoleon, or a representative of MI5?'

'He's given his name,' said the sergeant, 'as Mr S. D. Smith, solicitor of Rotherham.' He looked at me with raised eyebrows, as if to say, 'Sort that one out, pal.' I looked at him with raised eyebrows, as if to say, 'Fuck off!'

Geoffrey was sitting in his cell staring at the wall, quiet and contemplative. This worried me, as I didn't know what direction he was going to come from.

'Hello Geoffrey,' I said cautiously.

'I've told them I'm you,' he said boldly.

'Ah,' I said, smiling as if he were paying me a compliment. He laughed, so I laughed. He laughed some more, and so did I. It had the potential for being the funniest interview ever.

'You know what?' Geoffrey said thoughtfully. 'I think the system has it in for me. I think they'll get me in the end.'

For the first time, I saw that he was actually very vulnerable as well as stark staring mad, and I couldn't understand why nothing could be done. Of course Geoffrey was an unusual case, because he wasn't always mad, but I was convinced that Armley jail was no place for him. The reaction from a room full of jail-birds to the cry 'Hello, I'm the Earl of Scarborough' left little to the imagination. Though big and strong, the poor bugger would be no match for any group well-versed in the arts of tribal warfare.

The following day, my plea for bail fell on stony ground. In fairness to the court, they could do little else but remand him in custody: the over-burdened and under-funded Health Service had nowhere to put him; he had offended while on bail, and with serious offences, so it was a safe bet that if he were bailed he'd soon be back.

I wrote to the prison governor expressing my concerns, and he replied that Geoffrey had been transferred elsewhere, owing to 'certain problems' he had been causing on the wing. About three weeks after he was bailed, I saw Geoffrey in town, carrying a plastic bag full of shopping and talking to himself, which seemed to afford much amusement to the passers-by. I stopped to speak to him but he continued walking as if he hadn't seen me.

That afternoon, attending at court, I called to see the warrants officer to obtain the paperwork I needed. On the top of the pile of warrants on his desk was one bearing the name Geoffrey Samuel Plowright. It seemed that Geoffrey had been prosecuted for breaching his probation order and failing to comply with its requirements.

I told the warrants officer that he was a client of mine, and offered to see if I could persuade him to attend court. The warrants officer told me that, after a reasonable start to his probation order, Geoffrey had simply failed to turn up. Also, he hadn't been keeping his appointments with his psychiatrist, nor taken any of his medication.

I wrote to Geoffrey, inviting him to call to see me, or at least contact me to discuss the position, but never received a reply. I contacted the DSS, but he hadn't been signing on either. There appeared to be little I could do, so I forgot about him – until, three weeks later, I opened the *Rotherham Advertiser*. A headline screamed from the page: 'Local Man Found Hanged in his Home.'

I read the report, and there was Geoffrey's name. His body had been found when police went to the house to execute the warrant for his arrest; the report said that the pathologist believed he had been dead for about three weeks. There had been a suicide note, in which Geoffrey indicated that 'they' – whoever 'they' were – had got him in the end. He had signed it with his own name, and no reference to the Earl of Scarborough.

TWENTY

GOODBYE MOORGATE STREET, HELLO VICARAGE LANE

As Christmas 1982 approached, our search for new premises became a priority, but in the early 1980s, before the recession started, office space was soon snapped up. Eventually, we found two floors of offices on Vicarage Lane, overlooking All Saints Church and the grassed area surrounding it. It was in the centre of the town, and couldn't have been better placed, but unfortunately there were no parking facilities, and the open-plan floors needed considerable work to create private offices.

By the end of November, the office- and carpet-fitters moved out and we moved in. On the ground floor we had a reception area, off which led three interview rooms and three typing stations. Upstairs, our secretaries were set up outside our rooms, with me in the first room on the right, and Wilford next door, and we had a typing pool and two further offices, which we confidently agreed would be used for expansion. We were very proud of what we'd achieved, and decided to move into our new premises just before Christmas.

It was no small task to move ten people, ten sets of equipment and all the furniture we'd accumulated along the way. We also had eighteen months' worth of old files and all our current cases. We engaged the services of a friend and client of mine called Vito Lala, who had a removals firm. He and his colleagues did all the heavy work, while the rest of us pitched in to move our personal effects and some of the office equipment. The move took place over a weekend so as to cause the minimum disruption, but it was extremely stressful – particularly when we found that a couple of items were too large to be negotiated up the narrow staircase. However, a mixture of expertise, Broomie's hammer and brute force achieved the task by late Sunday, by which time the office was in total chaos.

Vito was world tea-drinking champion, and every so often there would be a little break for him to indulge in one of his favourite pastimes. Wilford, on the other hand, was world beer-drinking champion, even more impressive than the great Jarvis. (He later lost his title to 'Ten-Belly' Norburn, who in turn was beaten by the daddy of them all, Gary Webb, in the members' bar at Headingley during an England-Australia Test. Webbo consumed an astonishing thirty-five pints, though as he modestly pointed out, it was over an eighteen-hour session.) But on moving day, we were introduced to the Italian wine Lambrusco. Vito presented us with a bottle, assuring us that it wasn't particularly strong but had a very pleasant taste. It's not the sort of drink that will make you drunk, but the after-effects on the digestion are remarkable.

Searching for my desk drawers, I came across a number of boxed items labelled 'Jarvis'. They comprised a toaster, a box of onions, a large box of horse-racing magazines, an inflatable bed which on first sight looked like a blow-up doll, and a pot-bellied Buddha which I had presented to Jarvis the Christmas before for services rendered. I put them in one corner to be returned, except the Buddha, which adorns my office to this day.

We had spent a fortune on fittings, new carpets and decoration, and even bought a new telephone system described by British Telecom as 'Tomorrow's telephones today'. The representative told us, 'They're so refined they almost answer themselves,' but they never once did: success depended entirely on someone picking up the receiver. Wilf suggested we toast our new premises with a glass of Champagne, but unfortunately we didn't have any: two bottles of Mackeson had to suffice.

We were just finishing them when a scruffy little urchin walked into reception carrying a large cardboard box: apparently someone had given him a pound to make a special delivery. We opened the box to find a familiar ballcock, with a note that read, 'I hope this means as much to you as it means to me – Oscar'. We agreed to display it in the upstairs gents' toilet. As I hung it, I could have sworn I heard the sound of a distant trombone and the clatter of hooves.

One fixture that didn't move with us was the Space Invaders console; by then we were so busy that we didn't have time to play it, and had given it back to John Bradwell. We had a change of premises and also a change of attitude. The increase in staff increased our overheads, which meant we all had to work harder to cover our costs. The afternoon card games and entertaining chit-chat had disappeared as the pressure of work built up.

However, we still had the monthly meetings with Michael Jarvis, which usually involved a five-minute meeting dealing with the accounts followed by a four-hour session at a pub or restaurant; the dinner club's monthly nights out were eagerly awaited events, and the Wednesday football matches were a standard feature of the week. As to family – well, I have to admit they hardly saw me. There was always that serious case to deal with, clients who wouldn't wait, and the judge who had made an order for work to be done straight away. I had a mortgage and a firm to keep afloat, and of course the bank wanted to see money coming in, all of which took time. We did get some holidays, but only a few days at a time, because when I was off there was no one to cover the courts. Fortunately, Jennifer was busy with her singing and teaching career, and Rebecca was successful with her music festivals, which I always supported as best I could.

On the first Monday morning at Vicarage Lane, I was at my desk by 7.30am. At 8am the sign-writer came to print the firm's name in gold leaf on the large window above the entrance – it looked magnificent when it was finished. Just before nine the rest of the staff started to arrive, and with them came our first client in the new premises. Fittingly, it was Jack, and again he had Albert with him.

'By 'eck, it looks smart, Steve,' said Jack.

'Yes, we're very proud of it,' I replied.

Albert gave me his usual grin. I returned it. 'How are you, Albert?' I asked.

'Where's the fish?' demanded Albert.

'I'm not telling you,' I said.

'Don't worry, I'll find them,' he said.

'No,' I said, 'I don't want you running about, because we haven't got everything in place yet.'

'Let me have a look at the fish, Steve,' Albert pleaded, and Jack clouted him over the ear. Just then Morris, Jack's eldest son, walked into the office.

Apparently Morris had borrowed his father's Transit van and gone out for a ride when he spotted a stationary caravan, which he audaciously hooked onto the back of the Transit and drove off. Unfortunately, as he approached the M1 the Transit developed a mechanical fault, and he pulled into a lay-by to rectify it. As he was tinkering with the van, a motorist walked up to him carrying a petrol can, and asked, 'Could you run me to the petrol station?'

'No,' said Morris. 'Can't you see I'm busy?'

'I'm a member, and as I've broken down you're supposed to assist me.'

'Member of what?' said Morris.

The frustrated motorist pointed to the lettering on the side of the caravan. 'Here's my membership card, I've been in the AA for twenty years.'

'Oh,' said Morris, shamefaced, and added the first excuse that came into his head: 'Well, I'm only helping out because the regular man's got piles.'

The AA member realised there was something amiss, and stormed off to use his mobile phone. Morris didn't notice, and went on tinkering about with the Transit until the police arrived on the scene.

'Hello, hello,' said the police officer, 'and what have we got here, then? Is this your caravan, sir?'

'No,' said Morris, 'I'm looking after it for a friend.' He was escorted to the police car with a muscular arm on each of his shoulders.

Jack was livid. 'How could tha?' he demanded. 'And using the Transit, too!' he repeated time after time. 'Oh, the shame, how could tha do it?'

'Do wha'?' asked the pathetic Morris.

'Get caught!' said Jack. I managed to stand between them before they came to blows, and both parties apologised. Jack was many things, but at least he was well-mannered and never brought trouble or disorder to the office – apart from Albert, of course, who was nothing but trouble. As they left, I could hear the words, 'I nivver realised it were an AA caravan,' fading into the distance.

I set off for court with a smile on my face. The court corridor was packed, and most of the visitors were inspecting items of bed-linen they had obviously just bought. 'Oh no,' I thought, 'Jack's been at it again!'

He and Morris were in the WRVS canteen. 'You haven't nicked a load of bedding, have you?' I said as soon as I approached him.

'Who, me?' said Jack, wounded. 'Steve, would I?'

'Yes you bloody well would.'

'I'm not even up today, I've just come wi' 'im,' he said, looking at his son. I wasn't completely satisfied with the explanation, but left it at that, and we went to the 'rat hole' for a discussion. It was obvious that Morris should plead guilty to the charge, having admitted it to the police. Fortunately the AA had got their caravan back, so I had some mitigation to give to the court.

'If tha needs me as a character witness,' said Jack, 'I'm agreeable.'

'Thank you,' I said, 'I'll think about that, and if I need to call you, I will.' I couldn't help wondering what view the court might take of Jack as a character witness. I'd have got more credibility calling Al Capone.

I managed to call Morris on first, and the prosecutor opened his case. As I was about to get up to speak, Jack tapped me on the shoulder and whispered a last-minute instruction: 'Don't forget to tell them I'm a member of the RAC,' he said knowingly, and sat back in his seat. I'm still not sure of the relevance of that remark, or why it would be a point in mitigation.

The court adjourned the case for probation reports before sentencing, and the chairman of the magistrates said that he was looking at the possibility of community service work. 'Has he any particular skills?' he asked.

I was tempted to suggest car and caravan theft, but didn't think he'd appreciate it, so I said, 'No, sir, but he's a strong, healthy lad, and I'm sure the community service organiser will be able to find something for him to do.'

When I got back to the office late in the afternoon, the girls were busy decorating the Christmas tree, and soon after my arrival the lights were officially switched on. Apparently, Wilf had eaten two of the chocolate Santa Clauses and a marzipan reindeer, and drunk two of the miniature brandies.

The following day was Christmas Eve, and the office would close at lunchtime, after which there would be an office party before everyone left for Christmas. I had a very light court indeed, with only two cases, one an adjournment, and the other a prisoner who was lucky enough to secure bail for Christmas. I was back at the office at noon to sample some of the pork pie and sandwiches laid out for the party. We closed the office, and the guests began to arrive.

Bodger was first, followed by Tim Johnson from the building society and Mike Walker from Whitegate's estate agents, our neighbours. Soon the reception area was packed with people – all nearly deafened by the sound of a bugle being played rather badly outside. We took a vote on who it was, and the majority nominated Pagey.

Sure enough, the door burst open to reveal the man himself, wearing a Father Christmas robe, a German general's hat, and a dark toothbrush moustache – Adolf Hitler as Santa Claus.

'How do I look?' asked the Führer.

'A proper pillock,' I answered immediately.

'Thank you,' said Pagey. 'I thought it would be a success.'

Jarvis and the Mad Scotsman then appeared and bombarded Wilf and me with plastic string. We were really behaving like juveniles, but it was Christmas, and it didn't seem to matter. We presented Jarvis with a pink lavatory brush (this has become a tradition we continue to this day, and being the man he is, he hasn't thrown one of them away); I gave the speech and Wilford made the presentation, managing to remain upright throughout. The party ended at 2 o'clock and we adjourned to the Cross Keys, where the landlord had prepared a buffet for some of his regulars. Wilford entered a drinking competition with the Mad Scotsman, sixties' music blared from the jukebox, and the atmosphere was wonderful.

Just before 5pm I dragged myself away. I shook hands with everybody at least twice, and wandered off towards the taxi rank. As I passed the new office I saw the lights had been left on, so thought I should make sure the premises were secure.

In reception, the Christmas tree lights were flashing, and someone had removed Father Christmas from the top of the tree and put a Hitler doll there instead. There were empty beer cans on the reception counter and all the desks as well. Our smart new offices looked like the aftermath of a brewery trip.

I picked up some of the debris, including Pagey's bugle, which I attempted to blow; remarkably, I managed two notes. Going round turning off lights, and reflecting that an empty office at Christmas can be the loneliest place on earth, I was shaken from my thoughts by the voice of a small boy.

'Eh oop, Steve,' it said. 'I've been round once or twice, but there was no one 'ere.'

I turned round. 'Albert, what are you doing here?'

'I've come to see thee,' said Albert.

'But where's your dad?' I asked.

'Oh, I'm on me own, it's ma business,' said the little monster.

I sat on a reception chair and said, 'I can't stop long, Albert, I should have been away at 5 o'clock. Can't it wait till after Christmas?'

Albert sat down too, and treated me to one of his wide grins. I'd never really studied him closely, but then I noticed how like his father he was, that grin being the main distinguishing feature of their close-knit family. He was small for his age, probably due to genetics rather than undernourishment; his unkempt hair framed a cheeky face in which a pair of bright gentian-blue eyes contrasted with a dull, swarthy skin testifying to a lack of soap and water; and the grin, enhanced by the absence of central teeth and a preponderance of gum, gave him an almost comical appearance. He was actually rather ugly, yet there was something inexplicably striking about him. Intellectually he was 'Closed until further notice', but he was streetwise, and as Jack once said, ''E can 'old 'is own in a feight and 'e's nivver freetened to get stuck in. Mind thee, tha' 'ad to feight at oor 'ouse, wi' thirteen on us and only wun closet.'

Albert began, 'Tha sees, Steve, it's like this. Tha'll nivver believe it...'

And, do you know, he was right...